Gypsy Secrets

This book unveils the Romani secrets of fortune telling, explaining in detail the many different methods used by these nomads. For generations Gypsies have survived on their skills as seers. Their accuracy is legendary. They are a people who seem to be born with "the sight"…the ability to look into the past, present, and future using only the simplest of tools.

Penetrate the Lesser Mysteries as you learn obscure forms of fortune telling known only to a few. Here you will learn to read palms, to interpret symbols in a teacup, and to read cards—the Buckland Gypsy tarot, traditional tarot, and regular playing cards. You'll find out how to interpret the actions of animals, read the weather, and to instantly read a personality by the birthmarks (moles) and hands a person has.

Gypsies find many of their divination tools along the roadside or in the woods—others are easy to purchase at the local drugstore, the convenience store, or from the occasional traveling peddler. So gather together your Gypsy treasures—sticks and stones, knives and needles, cards and dice—and part the veil of mystery using the secrets that belong only to true Gypsy fortune tellers.

About the Author

Ray Buckland's grandfather was the first of the Buckland Gypsies to give up traveling the roads in a wagon and to settle in a permanent house. From his earliest years, Ray remembers listening to his father's and grandfather's tales of Romani life, and watching his grandmother read cards and tell fortunes. At an early age, Ray Buckland started his own serious study of the Old Knowledge and later came to write about it in a number of best-selling books. "Buckland" is a well-known name among English Gypsies, and Ray Buckland has become a well-known author of books on practical magic.

To Write to the Author

If you wish to contact the author or would like more information about this book, please write to the author in care of Llewellyn Worldwide, and we will forward your request. Both the author and publisher appreciate hearing from you and learning of your enjoyment of this book and how it has helped you. Llewellyn Worldwide cannot guarantee that every letter written to the author can be answered, but all will be forwarded. Please write to:

Raymond Buckland
c/o Llewellyn Worldwide
P.O. Box 64383, Dept. K092-2,
St. Paul, MN 55164-0383, U.S.A.

Please enclose a self-addressed, stamped envelope for reply, or $1.00 to cover costs. If outside the U.S.A., enclose international postal reply coupon.

GYPSY

Fortune Telling & Tarot Reading

Raymond Buckland

1998
Llewellyn Publications
St. Paul, Minnesota 55164-0383, U.S.A.

SECOND EDITION, Revised
First Printing, 1998
(Previously titled *Secrets of Gypsy Fortunetelling*)
First Edition published by Llewellyn Publications, 1988

Cover design by Lisa Novak.
Photos by Raymond Buckland.
Card illustrations by Raymond Buckland.
Illustrations on pages xii and 6 by Michelle Dillaire.
Book editing and design by Christine Nell Snow.

Library of Congress Cataloging-in-Publication Data
Buckland, Raymond.
    Gyspy fortune telling & tarot reading / Raymond Buckland. —
2nd ed.
        p.   cm.
    Rev. ed. of: Secrets of gypsy fortunetelling.
    ISBN 1-56718-092-2 (pbk.)
    1. Fortune-telling.   2. Tarot.   3. Gypsies—Folklore.
    I. Buckland, Raymond. Secrets of gypsy fortunetelling.
    II. Title.
BF1874.B83   1998
133.3'089'91497—dc21   98-12173
                                                             CIP

PUBLISHER'S NOTE:
Llewellyn Worldwide does not participate in, endorse, or have any authority or responsibility concerning private business transactions between our authors and the public. All mail addressed to the author is forwarded but the publisher cannot, unless specifically instructed by the author, give out an address or phone number.

Llewellyn Publications
A Division of Llewellyn Worldwide, Ltd.
P.O. Box 64383, Dept. K092-2
St. Paul, Minnesota 55164-0383

Printed in the U. S. A.

Other Books by Raymond Buckland

Advanced Candle Magick (Llewellyn, 1996)

Buckland Gypsies' Domino Divination Deck (Llewellyn, 1995)

Ray Buckland's Magic Cauldron (Galde Press, 1995)

Truth About Spirit Communication (Llewellyn, 1995)

Doors to Other Worlds (Llewellyn, 1993)

The Book of African Divination (Inner Traditions, 1992)

Scottish Witchcraft (Llewellyn, 1991)

Secrets of Gypsy Dream Reading (Llewellyn, 1990)

Secrets of Gypsy Love Magick (Llewellyn, 1990)

Buckland's Complete Book of Witchcraft (Llewellyn, 1986)

Practical Color Magick (Llewellyn, 1983)

The Magic of Chant-O-Matics (Parker, 1978)

Anatomy of the Occult (Weiser, 1977)

Amazing Secrets of the Psychic World—with Hereward
   Carrington (Parker, 1975)

Here Is the Occult (House of Collectibles, 1974)

The Tree: Complete Book of Saxon Witchcraft (Weiser, 1974)

Witchcraft from the Inside (Llewellyn, 1971, 1975, 1995)

Mu Revealed—writing as Tony Earll (Warner, 1970)

Practical Candleburning Rituals (Llewellyn, 1970,1976, 1982)

Witchcraft Ancient and Modern (House of Collectibles, 1970)

A Pocket Guide to the Supernatural (Ace, 1969)

Witchcraft...the Religion (Buckland Museum, 1966)

Fiction

Cardinal's Sin (Llewellyn, 1995)

The Committee (Llewellyn, 1993)

Video

Witchcraft Yesterday and Today (Llewellyn, 1990)

*For my parents and grandparents
—Stanley and Lizzie Buckland;
Bert and Alice Buckland—
and for all Buckland Travelers*

• ∽ •

Contents

Preface to the Second Edition

Gypsies seem to be a never ending fascination to many people. Their skill at fortune telling is especially intriguing. How is it that they are so successful? If it was all fake, all charlatanism, then surely they would not have been able to keep up the pretense generation after generation, for many hundreds of years.

With the publication of *Secrets of Gypsy Fortunetelling* in 1988, I, as a half-blood Gypsy myself, was able to demonstrate that these divinatory practices are not charlatanism. I was able to show that anyone—

with practice—can do card reading and crystal ball gazing, can read palms, dice, and dominoes; anyone can do and enjoy the many divination practices of the Gypsies.

Now it is time to enlarge that book; to incorporate in it further card reading—specifically the use of the Buckland Gypsy Fortune Telling Tarot. This is a deck that was devised and used by the Buckland Gypsies at a time when regular tarot cards were not easy to come by. I never saw my grandmother without the deck in her hands. It seemed to me, as a child, that she used it all day and every day. She read for family, friends and neighbors, strangers, and even for herself.

Some of the spreads that were used by my family, and by other Gypsies, have been included in this new edition of the book. They give a rich variety to what you may offer as a card reader.

Along with the new card material, I have reviewed and, where necessary, revised the other material, making *Gypsy Fortune Telling and Tarot Reading* an indispensible book for the teller of fortunes, whatever his or her previous experience. I hope you read, learn, and enjoy the Gypsies' way of *dukkerin'* (fortune telling).

—Raymond Buckland
1998

Introduction

I am what is known as a *poshrat* or half-blood Romani (from *posh*—half; *ratti*—blood). My father was a full-blood. My grandfather was the first of the family to settle into a permanent dwelling and give up the traveling ways *jalling a drom* in a *vardo*. There are old photographs of Buckland Gypsies and their waggons in such books as *The Gypsies—Waggon-Time and After* by Denis Harvey (Batsford, 1979), *The English Gypsy Caravan* by C. H. Ward-Jackson and Denis E. Harvey (David and Charles, 1973), and in *Making Model Gypsy Caravans* by John

Thompson (Thompson, 1978). Charles Godfrey Leland also mentions a Buckland Gypsy in his *Gypsy Sorcery and Fortune-Telling* (Fisher-Unwin, 1891).

To many, the Gypsies have always seemed a mysterious people, mainly because they tend to keep very much to themselves and have a distrust of *gaujos*, or non-Gypsies. The Gypsies—or, to give them their true name, the *Rom* (Romani)—have always been well versed in occult lore and have been particularly adept at divination, or fortune-telling. Indeed, they were responsible for bringing with

Illustration by Michelle Dillaire.

A shuvani working Romani magic.

them much of our present knowledge of this field, in their migration from the East, and through their travels they have spread this knowledge.

One of the things that has helped keep the *Rom* insulated from the many peoples and countries through which they have traveled is language. They have their own language: Romanes. It has certainly changed over the centuries, and in different countries many local words have been picked up and added to it. But the basics have remained enough that a Gypsy from one country can usually manage to talk with a Gypsy from any other country. The *Rom* words I include in this book are English Romanes, or *poggerdi jib*.

There are many Sanskrit words, or words derived from Sanskrit, in Romanes, which is another indication of the origin of the *Rom*.

Dukkerin' is the Romani word for fortune telling (there is an older word, *drabbering*, but that is not used, or even much known, today). Although literally meaning "hand reading" (*duk*=hand), *dukkerin'* is used for all forms of divination: reading palms, cards, and tea leaves; throwing dice; crystal gazing; and interpreting omens and portents. Whatever its form, however, *dukkerin'* is of a PRACTICAL nature in that the Gypsy utilizes nothing more complex than, for example, a deck of cards, a cup of tea, a bunch of sticks, or a set of dice—all easily obtainable items of no great worth in themselves.

My grandfather read palms and was an expert at interpreting the actions of birds and animals. My grandmother, a true *Shuvani* (Wise Woman), favored the cards. Both were very psychic themselves and could function well without any tools, yet they both knew that "props" could be useful. Basically they serve as a focal point and as a means of graphically illustrating what needs to be emphasized…turn over the "Death" card in a tarot deck and you'll really capture the attention of the person you're reading for!

The Gypsies, more than any other people, were responsible for the interest in, and perfection of, the divinatory arts, promoting them and spreading them—as the Gypsies themselves spread—across Asia and Europe, then into the New World. Let's look for a moment at the history of these travelers.

• ☙ •

1

The Coming
of the Gypsies

Somewhere around the mid-ninth century a large group of people left their homeland in the north of India and moved westward. What prompted this initial move we do not know, but it was the start of a wave of dark-skinned nomads that grew in number and swarmed across Asia and Europe.

According to the Gypsy writer Petulengro (*A Romany Life*, Methuen, 1935):

> ...through Afghanistan and Persia they came, reaching the Caspian Sea (to the north of the Persian Gulf). They had split into different bands earlier. The northern tribe went up

the Euphrates and Tigris. Then some went to the Black Sea and others to Syria, but the majority went to Turkey. Another tribe went through Palestine and Egypt. The southern group went along the north Africa coast until they came to Gibraltar and crossed into Spain. The branch that passed through Turkey crossed the Bosporus, into Greece and the Balkans, and from there into Central Europe.

By 1417 there were Gypsies in Germany; by 1430 they had reached England. By the time they reached western Europe, the Gypsies carried with them seemingly authentic "Letters of Protection" from various rulers, including Sigismund, King of the Romans (actually King of Hungary) and even Pope Martin V. On the basis of these letters, initially they were generally well received. It was a time when the Church had elevated charity into a virtue, so charity was universally extended to these colorful vagrants.

Various stories circulated concerning the travelers. A common one was that they were living out a seven-year penance imposed on them because of their paganism. However, they would temporarily settle in an area and happily live off the sympathetic charity for many times the seven years. They gradually came to be regarded as part of the so-called "dangerous classes." Jean-Paul Clébert (in *Les Tsiganes*, 1961) quotes the "General Inventory of the History of Thieves" that said:

> …to be considered as an outstanding robber, it was necessary to have passed through (or graduated from) the "Beggars' Republic"; to know all the tricks and wiles and activities of the Gypsies; to be acquainted with the various groups within that organization…

This was the beginning of the persecutions from which the Gypsy people still have not freed themselves.

The sudden arrival of thousands of these people was enough to cause consternation in many of the countries they "invaded." They became a major social problem. In much of the West, the reaction was persecution. King Ferdinand of Spain was the first to take specific action. In 1492 he banished Gypsies. Any who would not leave were to be exterminated. Again to quote Clébert:

A "Reading" style Gypsy vardo.

People of fixed residence, at one and the same time suspicious and credulous, regarded all those of itinerant occupations who had no settled abode and came from distant countries as possessed of the evil eye…every stranger was suspect; all the more if he had a swarthy face, wore rings in his ears, lived in wheeled houses, and spoke a language which was obviously not a Christian one.

The Gypsies were equated with Witches and Sorcerers. They were accused of engaging in black magic and dealing with the Devil. The Parliament of Paris, in 1539, recorded an expulsion order, and in 1560, the States General of Orléans called on "all those impostors known by the name of Bohemians or Egyptians to leave the kingdom under penalty of the galleys." In 1607, Henri IV renewed the expulsion order.

But in fact these expulsion orders had a small effect and the Gypsies continued practicing their crafts, albeit under a state of persecution. This persecution has continued through to the present. In the World War II, almost half a million Gypsies were gassed, shot, or hanged in the Nazi concentration camps, yet this is today seldom remembered or remarked upon.

In Britain and America the Gypsies continue to be hounded, and their nomadic lifestyle is looked upon as somehow antagonistic to "the system." But the Gypsies, the *Rom*, doggedly refuse to conform. They see no reason to be forced to change their lifestyle of centuries if they can possibly get away with it. They continue to *jal a drom* (travel the road) as wandering peddlers, musicians, dancers, dealers in all things, and tellers of fortunes. I hope they always will.

• ∾ •

2

Dukkerin'

Among the Gypsies there are four favorites for *dukkerin'*. They are the palm, tea leaves, the crystal, and cards (not necessarily in that order). I'll look at these first and then go on to some of the other methods employed, including several that are little known in the world of the *gaujo*, or non-Gypsy.

One thing needs to be kept in mind when doing readings: that is, that most people do take them seriously. Even those who outwardly profess to laugh at the very idea of being able to see any indication of future events do, unconsciously

Dukkerin' a gaujo.

perhaps, take your words to heart. Because of this you should be very careful in what you say. For example, if you should see death in your client's future, do *not* say, "Oh! You're going to die!" Always choose your words carefully, stressing the necessity to be extra careful or to pay particular attention to their health at certain times, rather than boldly stating that there will be an accident or that they will suffer some dreadful disease. As much as possible, try to stress the *good* things. Don't forget that we create our own realities; that what you see indicated in the cards, the palm, or wherever, is only an indication of what is likely to happen with the forces currently in play. The future *can* be changed. We do have freedom of choice. If, then, you stress the favorable aspects, you will set the person's mind toward creating what he or she really wants to happen. The rest is then up to them.

One further point: it is quite possible, and permissible, to read for yourself. Yes, you can read your own palm, your own cards, your own tea leaves, etc. There is nothing wrong in that at all. You may well tend to read into it things that you are aware of, or things that you would like to see (wishful thinking), and to ignore those things you don't want to see! However, by reading on a regular basis you will be able to overcome this tendency to a large extent. So, don't listen to anyone who says that you can't, or shouldn't, read for yourself.

• ᴄᴈ •

3

Hand Reading

The Gypsy palmist is always an attraction, whether at carnivals, "tea rooms," or through chance encounters—always the center of attention. Using the palm of the hand as a focal point, the Gypsy palmist can tell all of your past, present, and future with seemingly uncanny accuracy. Is there a trick to this? No. The only "trick" is in learning the meanings of the various lines, mounts, divisions, and types of hand.

General Observations

What makes the lines in your hands? It's the way in which we use them. The major lines of the hands are caused by the folding of the palm and the activity of the fingers. The heavy, resisting hand will be less lined than the flexible one, and so also will "heavy" natures be less influenced by others and surroundings than will more delicate natures.

What determines *type*? The makeup of the whole body gives the type of hand. We seldom see hands completely at variance with the rest of the body, though it can happen on occasion. An example would be the "inherited" hand… much as we find a family nose, or family jaw, so can we find a family hand. Another exception is the person who keeps a very conscious division between actual desires and aptitudes and his or her place in the world. Such a person is either leading a double life or is so secretive that it amounts to a mania (such secretive people must be consciously or unconsciously aware that their hands give them away and instinctively tend to keep their hands tightly closed, as though in an effort to hide their palms).

The hand is individual at birth and changes with life's vicissitudes. The condition of the palm reveals a great deal. Nervousness, for example, shows itself in several ways: an over-moist palm; a super-dry one; or it has a spottiness—an underskin seemingly patched by dark and light dots.

The hand that is cold and dry needs attention; the circulation is imperfect. If it is hot and dry, the nerves need relaxing (intestinal disorders often show up this way).

The knottiness of rheumatism shouldn't be mistaken for the heavy joints of temper. The former is nubby; the latter has a more even thickness at the joint.

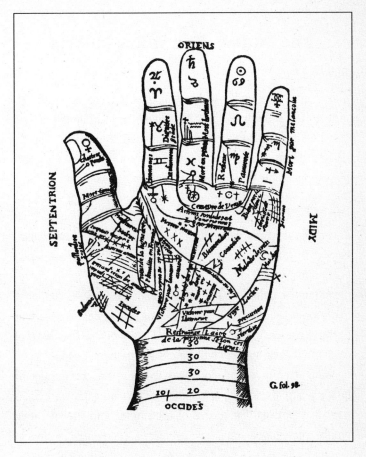

**The signs of the Zodiac and their positions
on the hand.**

(From Jean Baptiste Belot's Œuvres of 1640.)

I have talked with many Gypsies on the subject of palm reading. The following is a compilation of all they have told me.

The Outline, Fingers and Mounts

Short Hands

Short hands generally indicate a tendency to be quick to judge. If with pointed fingers, then the judgment may be aided by imagination, but the overall picture only will be considered. Short, knotty fingers (with large joints) indicate good reasoning on the whole, but a failure to analyze in any detail.

Long Hands

Long hands show a capacity for detail. If very large also, they will overdo it. Long fingers show feeling and susceptibility and, when pointed, tact.

When the palm is much longer than the fingers, and large in proportion, the capacity for detail is lessened. There will be little capacity for very fine, delicate work, either mental or manual. The subject will be easily satisfied.

When the fingers are longer than the palm, the mind will be very active and the spirit of criticism and contradiction strong. There will be a love of argument, and the memory will be very good.

Equal Hands

When the palm and fingers are of equal length, the balance will be perfect, with good judgment and instinct.

Hard Hands

These show energy and perseverance. If hard and pointed, activity with elegance. If excessively hard, however, there is an indication of some lack of intelligence.

Soft Hands

These show laziness of mind and/or body. Soft and spatulate indicate an active mind but a lazy body; soft and square, the reverse. It should be noted, however, that here there is nothing to do with the skin, which may be hardened by the subject's occupation or softened by lack of manual labor. The softness of the hand here dealt with is a judgment based on the *consistency* when pressed.

Supple fingers show quick action and versatility. Very thick hands show selfishness and self-esteem.

Skin

When the hand is soft and the skin very lined, the subject will be impressionable. If hard and lined, quarrelsome. All hands covered with many small lines show either an agitated life or ill health. A very white hand, which does not change with heat and cold, is a sign of selfishness.

Nails

The nails, and the ends of the fingers, show the temper of the subject (the lines have also to be considered, but more on that below). Short and square nails show a fighting temper. If wider than they are long, obstinacy. If square at the bottom instead of curved, passionate anger. Short nails, even with a hand otherwise benevolent, show criticism and contradiction.

Very large nails, curved at the bottom, indicate a good head for business. If they flush pink at the outer edges, there may be occasional fits of irritation. Thin nails are an indication of delicate health.

When nails are ridged and hard there is a condition of health that needs looking into; it might be undernourishment or intestinal disorder. Bad circulation will produce a blueness. Hard and brittle nails show a lack of oil and mineral salts in the system.

Fingers

The fingers are generally divided into three classes: pointed, square and spatulate (the class is more easily judged from looking at the back of the hand rather than the front). Sometimes you will find a mixture. For example, a hand may have a pointed first finger while the others are square. For this reason, let's look at each of the fingers and the thumb separately (see illustration).

The phalanges of the fingers are counted from the top— the first phalange being the one with the nail.

Thumb

The thumb, ruled by Venus and concerned with love, is the most important feature of the whole hand. The character of the subject depends a great deal on it.

lst Phalange: Will

2nd Phalange: Reason

3rd Phalange: Love

First Phalange: Long and strong—energetic will, self confidence, love of perfection. A person of will. Medium—passive resistance. Short—changeableness, inconsistency.

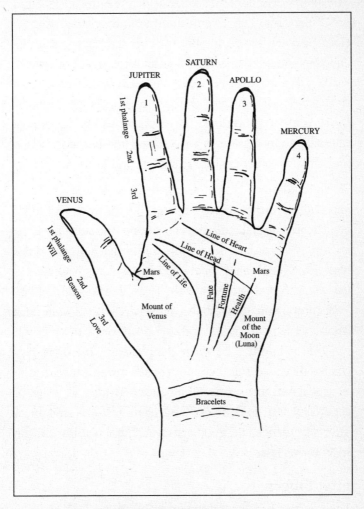

**The hand, showing major lines and mounts;
fingers and their associations.**

Second Phalange: This should be a little longer than the first and should be rather thick. When the first and second are of the same length, and the thumb is relatively longer than the other fingers, it indicates a very strong and sensible character. If the same thumb is only of medium length, there will be no rule over others but passive resistance and a strong and wise character. With the first phalange short and the second long and thick, the character will be reasonable but liable to indecision. A good strong first phalange with a long thick second may lead to success and fortune.

Third Phalange: This is also called the Mount of Venus and will be further discussed later. If very thick and high, encroaching onto the middle of the hand, the subject will be governed by passion. If medium and in harmony with the rest of the hand, affectionate and benevolent. If weak and flat, cold-hearted and (unless the Heart line is good) selfish.

A thumb too short shows indecisiveness. If wide and heavy at the point, it will indicate obstinacy, particularly if the joint is knotty. The wider the phalange, the more pig-headed the subject! If the thumb bends inwards towards the fingers, it indicates avarice. If it bends outwards, it's a sign of generosity and, sometimes, extravagance. If it is straight, it means prudence and good sense. A thumb set low on the hand shows talent.

First Finger

The finger of Jupiter, and the finger of Justice.

This should be long relative to the other fingers and it should be straight.

Pointed: Indicates quick apprehension, intuition, love of reading.

Square: Love of truth.

Spatulate: (very rare) Error, exaggerated action. If pointed when the other fingers are square, serious thought and artistic talent.

First Phalange Long: Religion.

Second Phalange Long: Ambition.

Third Phalange Long: Pride; love of rule.

All Phalanges Short: Want of thought; little contemplation.

Second Finger

The finger of Saturn, and the finger of Success.

Pointed: Frivolity, carelessness.

Square: Prudence, grave character, sadness.

Spatulate: Activity, superstition.

First Phalange Long: Melancholy.

Second Phalange Long: Love of agriculture.

Third Phalange Long: Avarice.

All Phalanges Short: Devious; sly.

Third Finger

The finger of Apollo, and the finger of Art, Fame, and Riches.

Pointed: Artistic feeling and intuition. If with all of the others in opposition, frivolity and boasting.

Square: Truth and reason in art and in life.

Spatulate: Love of form, of movement in art, dramatic talent. Many actors have this finger, and in artists it signifies painters of animal or genre subjects.

First Phalange Long: Love of art and color.

Second Phalange Long: Love of work.

Third Phalange Long: Love of display, vanity, desire to shine, love of riches.

All Phalanges Short: Capricious; a dilettante.

Fourth Finger

The finger of Mercury, and the finger of affection.

It is good that this finger should be straight and long, and if the subject would "turn others around his or her little finger," then it should rise above the first knot of the third finger.

Pointed: Eloquence, tact, diplomacy. There is, however, a leaning towards trickery if excessively pointed.

Square: Reason in science, love of the abstract, good at teaching, good at business.

Spatulate: Mechanical skill, love of machinery. If excessively spatulate, it indicates a tendency towards theft.

First Phalange Long: Love of talking, eloquence, skill.

Second Phalange Long: Industry, common sense, good at business, love of argument.

Third Phalange Long: Scheming, lying.

All Phalanges Short: Frugal; penny-pinching.

If, when the hands are held open and loose, the first and second fingers fall naturally widest apart, it shows independence of thought. If the third and fourth are widest, independence of action. If both are very wide, great originality and self-reliance. If the fingers naturally curl up towards the palm when so held, the subject will be conventional.

When the third phalanges of all fingers are thick at the root, it is a sign of greediness, or at least a love of good things to eat and drink. When the third phalanges of all the fingers incline downwards below the mounts, it shows shyness and, sometimes extreme cowardice. If the first phalanges are hollow and curve upwards—avarice. Reversed—extravagance.

If the thumb inclines inwards—avarice and selfishness; outwards—generosity.

It should be noted that the inclination of the fingers towards each other requires a lot of study. No one seems to have studied this aspect sufficiently. The few rules outlined above are the ones used by most Romani, but it seems there is still much to be learned on this point.

The Mounts

As with the lines, the meaning of the mounts (lying at the base of the fingers and thumb) may be modified by other indications in the hand. The qualities listed are those associated with that particular mount. If the mount seems especially full and fleshy, then consider the listing "Excess." If however, the mount seems especially flat and lacking in flesh, then consider the listing "Absence."

Mount of Jupiter (First Finger)

Qualities: Religion, ambition, honor, gaiety, love of society. A good Mount of Jupiter will always show a great mind.

Excess: Pride, love of power, domineering, conceit, superstitious.

Absence: Irreligious, selfishness, idleness, want of dignity, vulgarity.

Mount of Saturn (Second Finger)

Qualities: Prudence, wisdom.

Excess: Taciturnity, sadness, love of solitude.

Absence: Misfortune, insignificance in life.

Mount of Apollo (Third Finger)

Qualities: Love of art or literature, genius, intelligence, hope, calm, beauty and grace of mind, gentleness, toleration, mercy.

Excess: Love of money, extravagance, curiosity, boasting, scoffing, lying, envy.

Absence: Dullness, insignificance.

Mount of Mercury (Fourth Finger)

Qualities: Cheerfulness, intelligence, wit, eloquence, industry, inventiveness, promptness of action and thought, love of work.

Excess: Lying, theft, treachery, ruse, trickery, pretentiousness, ignorance.

Absence: Want of intelligence and aptitude, negativity.

Mount of Mars

There are two Mounts of Mars. One is beneath the Mount of Jupiter, divided from it by the Line of Life, and the other is beneath the Mount of Mercury, divided from it by the Line of Heart. The Plain of Mars lies between the two.

Qualities of the first (beneath Jupiter): Active, courage, presence of mind, resolution, aggressiveness.

Excess: Great courage, dash and daring, love of danger for its own sake.

Absence: Cowardice, timidity, want of presence of mind.

Qualities of the second (beneath Mercury): Passive courage, devotion, self-command, resignation, strength of resistance, noble pride.

Excess: Great fortitude, calm strength, power of forgiveness.

Absence: Cowardice, timidity, want of presence of mind.

Note: For both mounts, when the Excess is together with negative lines, it can mean cruelty, tyranny, blood-thirstiness, anger, injustice, and insolence; study these mounts very carefully and read them in conjunction with the lines (as you should do with all mounts, of course).

Mount of Venus (Thumb)

Qualities: Beauty, grace, affection, charity, benevolence; love of beautiful things, of dancing, of melody in music; desire of pleasing, and the pleasures of the senses.

Excess: Inconstancy, effrontery, coquetry, vanity, idleness, sensuality.

Absence: Coldness, selfishness, want of tenderness and love.

Note: If the mount is flat, there is a want of the qualities. With a hard hand, a much-developed mount will give wit and grace of manner, and will counteract the melancholy of a developed Mount of Saturn.

Mount of Luna

This is found on the outside of the hand, beneath the Mount of Mars and opposite that of Venus.

Qualities: Imagination, sentiment, refinement, poetry, harmony in music, love of scenery.

Excess: Despair, discontent, caprice, irritability, sadness, superstition.

Absence: Dullness, want of sympathy, of imagination, of ideas, severe judgment of others.

The mounts should always be judged with due regard for the shape of the fingers, otherwise there is a danger of confusing positive and negative qualities. It is also very necessary to study and understand the lines. For example, a straight Line of Head, a poor Line of Heart, knotted fingers, and a long first phalange of the thumb will give to a fine Line of Apollo love of money instead of art; the subject will be a speculator, not an artist. Look also to see if idleness (soft hand) will not prevent success. Look also to see if the mounts incline towards each other. If Mercury encroaches on Apollo, science will join art; if towards the "percussion" or outside of the hand, it will show a talent for business. Mars inclining towards Mercury will denote courage in free speech and energy in the management of affairs. Mars towards Luna, energy in imagination, and so on.

Time

Time is counted downwards on the Line of Life and also downwards on the Line of Head. Contrarily, on the Line of Fate, time is counted upwards from the wrist to the Mount of Saturn. This is also the case with the Line of Fortune. On the Line of Heart, it is counted from the Mount of Jupiter to the percussion of the hand.

The Lines

Line of Life (Vital)

The Line of Life concerns itself literally with the matter of physical being. It extends around the thumb at the place where the thumb of a glove would be sewn on.

The Line of Life shows the length of the subject's existence and health or illness during the period. Time is measured on it, and the incidents marked on the other lines are corroborated.

The Line of Life should be long, narrow, deep, softly colored, and completely encircling the Mount of Venus. This will indicate long life, without illness, and a good character.

Signs of Illness: If the line is pale and very deep: bad health. Small dark clots on it: nervous illness. Small lines crossing it: small illnesses, generally headaches. Chained and uneven: painful life, bad health. Stopping suddenly with a dark dot: death by accident or violence. Broken in one hand and weak in the other: a serious illness. Broken in both hands: probable death. Forked at the end: possible insanity—where this is found it is good to caution the subject against overwork, either mentally or physically. It is always a bad sign and a serious warning.

Branches: When branch lines rise on either side of the Line of Life, it shows riches and dignity; if they fall downwards, it indicates poverty or loss of character. If the Life Line is divided and one branch goes away onto the Mount of Luna and deepens, it shows long voyages and distant traveling. Cross lines—many very small cross lines: ill health and delicate constitution. Lines from the Mount of Venus crossing the Line of Life are misfortunes caused by other people.

Attendant Lines: When the Line of Life is closely followed by another line, which may occasionally intertwine itself with it, it's a sign of great vigor and success and a promise of riches. Lines further off from the Line of Life, which follow its course more or less regularly, represent the influence of other people over the subject's life. Their intensity and duration may be calculated by their depths and by the nearness of their approach to the Line of Life.

Stars and Crosses: Near the Line of Life, these can indicate trouble. It is often an infirmity from which the subject may not recover. When the Vital Line ends in a series of crosses, the subject may have an amiable character and talent, but if the crosses are found in both hands, the subject will never succeed in anything great in life.

Line of Head (Cerebral)

This should be even, long, and narrow. This will show strong judgment, determined will, and clear mind. If the Mount of Mercury is much developed, there will be originality and energy. If Mercury is low, more learning and less ability.

When the line is separated from the Line of Life, this is a sign of self-confidence, and when found in both hands, sometimes conceit. Such subjects can be impulsive and should be warned against acting hastily.

When the Line of Head is joined to the Line of Life, this is a sign of a need for self-confidence. If it is joined as far as the middle of both hands, timidity and moral cowardice will be excessive. Unless there are signs of very great talent, such subjects will never succeed at anything.

When the line is very long and straight, this is a sign of common sense, of care and economy. If it goes straight, right across the hand, however, it indicates avarice, selfishness, and greed. But this need not be the case if the other signs are very good in the hand—with a fine Mount of Jupiter, a turned-out thumb, and a good Line of Heart.

When the line is very long and sloping, this is a sign of imagination, artistic feeling, poetry, but little judgment. In excess it will bring much folly and delusion, especially if the Mount of Luna is much developed and lined.

When the Line of Head is forked, this is a good sign. In fact it is a good sign for any line to be forked, with the exception of the Line of Life. When the Head Line ends in a small fork, it shows both imagination and common sense. Should the fork be large, it indicates a tendency to trickery and/or diplomacy! The subject may deceive him or herself, but also has the ability to deceive others.

When the line is short and only advances to the middle of the hand, it shows a want of spirit, dash, and balance. The subject will see only one side of any question. If it stops under the Mount of Saturn, life will be short and death sudden.

When the line is chained, it shows a want of fixity in ideas; there is too much variety. But if the line is followed throughout by another sister line, it often indicates a great inheritance.

Line of Heart (Mensal)

This should be narrow and deep, of a good color, and running straight from the Mount of Jupiter to the Mount of Mercury. This indicates a good heart; strong and happy affection. The longer the Heart Line, the nobler and more ideal the love. But should the line completely encircle the Mount of Jupiter, and the Head Line slope on Luna, the subject may make him or herself unhappy with jealousy.

When the line is short, not rising until beneath the Mount of Saturn, it is a sign of a cold heart. With a very long Head Line and strong thumb, the subject will be very constant, even though the Heart Line is short. This will make the subject affectionate to the few he or she loves, though lacking in general love to humankind.

When the line is forked, a fork under Jupiter is a true sign of trustworthiness and constancy, but not of happiness in love. The more even the fork, the more ideal the character.

Branches rising and falling from the Line of Heart show the influence of other people on the affections. A branch that rises high on the Mount of Jupiter promises great happiness and successful ambition, if uncrossed. When a branch cuts through the line and descends beneath it, it is a sign of disappointment. When there are many branches, it is a sign that the feelings of love and hate are very strong. No branches mean a loveless life so far as the opposite sex is concerned.

A break in the Line of Heart generally means a broken engagement, or great disappointment, with regard to a person loved.

Dots and dents on the Heart Line show troubles, both physical and mental. When the dot is red, the sorrow has been very keen. White dots are conquests in love. Black or blue ones are signs of shock or illness.

When the line is chained, or has islands, it indicates inconstancy, caprice, flirtation, and intrigue. It sometimes even indicates contempt for the opposite sex.

Line of Fate (Saturnian)

This shows worldly success or failure, and the general course of the life. There are four principal places for the departure of this line:

From the Line of Life: This is good and common. The line then partakes of the life-qualities, shows a generous heart, and if uncrossed, shows prosperity and happiness.

From the Plain of Mars: (Middle of the hand.) This will show a life of trouble. But there is also hope and energy. There will always be struggles and obstacles, but if success is achieved, it will be by merit alone.

From the Bracelet: This will show a fine and uncommon destiny, if found in both hands. If it goes from the Bracelet to the Mount of Saturn, ending high up on it, it shows great success (and still more certain if the line is forked). If it passes over the mount and enters the Finger of Saturn, it shows a great destiny. However, should it mount still higher and end in a star, it is said to presage a heroic career ending in violence, or a great crime!

From the Mount of Luna: When the Line of Fate rises from here, it shows that all the happiness of the life will arise from the actions of some other person(s). Destiny is taken out of the hands of the subject altogether. If a Luna Line of Fate stops at the Heart Line, and there is a well-formed cross on the Mount of Jupiter, fortune and happiness will come through a good marriage.

If the line rises from below the Bracelet, it shows a very bad influence of fate and great grief.

When the Fate Line is broken, it does not necessarily mean misfortune. If the line continues again, after the break, well marked and uncrossed, it will probably indicate a great event in the life. And if the lines run parallel for a little distance, the event may bring a change for the better in position and dignity.

When chained with a double line, it is a sign of misfortune, bad character, and unhappiness brought about by evil deeds.

Branches upwards from the Fate Line show improvement in position and wealth, but if they tend downwards, there will be reversals and possible poverty.

In studying the Line of Fate, both hands should be carefully compared.

Line of Fortune (Solar)

This shows glory, fame and riches, artistic and literary talent; success, worldly distinction, and prosperity. It should be narrow, deep, straight, long, and rise high on the Mount of Apollo. There are four places from which the line may rise:

From the Line of Life: This is very favorable and will show success and fortune gained by inheritance or by merit. The lower the line rises, the more surely will honor or celebrity be attained.

From the Mount of Luna: In this case, success or fortune will be gained unexpectedly and by the help of other people.

From the Plain of Mars: (Middle of the hand.) In this case, success will come late in life, or towards middle-age, and will be the result of personal merit and exertion.

From the Line of the Heart: This will show an appreciative character, a love of art and the beautiful; but neither wealth nor fame will be gained by it.

Cross lines are obstacles in the way of success. If they bar the line near the beginning, they will show loss of fortune by parents during youth.

A single fork on the Mount of Apollo will show success in one line of life. But if there are many forks, there will be taste and talent in many different branches of art, politics, or literature, but with energy being too widely distributed, nothing will be brought to success or perfection.

Unless there is a good Mount of Jupiter, a Line of Apollo cannot bring much success except in the shape of money.

The Line of Health (Hepatica)

It is a sign of a very strong constitution to be without this line. This Line of Health should start from the Bracelet, or from the Line of Life, and go on or towards the Mount of Mercury. It is very irregular and may begin or end almost anywhere in the hand. It should be long, narrow, clear, well-colored, and straight. This will show good health, good memory, and a kind heart. If the line is tortuous, it indicates a bad temper.

A cross on the line shows an illness, the date of which must be looked for on the Line of Life. Small lines crossing it show weakness and delicacy, often headaches and neuralgia.

The Line of Intuition (Line of Luna)

This is not a very common line and is, as a rule, only found on imaginative or intellectual hands. It should rise on or beneath the Mount of Luna and proceed in a sort of half-circle onto or towards the Mount of Mercury.

If it is clear, straight, and narrow, it indicates intuition and ability to hypnotize and read others' thoughts. The subject will have a taste for the occult; for divination, clairvoyance, etc. If there is an island near the beginning of the line, there is the gift of second sight. If the line is branched, tortuous, or short, there will be danger of caprice and over-imagination, possibly even leading eventually to lunacy.

When the Line of Luna forms a triangle with the Line of Fate and the Line of the Head, it is said to indicate a good palm reader. An island on the line shows a tendency to somnambulism.

The Ring of Venus

This is a half-circle formed by a line starting from between the first and second fingers, crossing or surrounding the Mounts of Saturn and Apollo, and ending (when perfect) between the third and fourth fingers. This is generally considered a line of misfortune, since it breaks both the Line of Fate and the Line of Fortune and cuts off the Mounts of Saturn and Apollo.

The Lesser Lines

The Plain of Mars

This is in the center of the palm of the hand; the valley through which the Line of Head flows. If it is high, it shows aggressiveness and daring. If low, the subject will never rise to any high position. The lines and signs marked on the

Plain of Mars are considered under the headings of the Quadrangle and the Triangle.

The Quadrangle: This is the space between the Line of Heart and the Line of Head. If it is wide and regular, largest nearest the percussion, and the lines bounding it of good color, it shows justice, loyalty, and broad, tolerant views; a straightforward and courageous character. Should it be narrow, it shows narrow views and conventionality; a tendency to injustice and indecision. In an otherwise good hand, but with a weak Line of Health, it often indicates asthma.

When the narrowness of the Quadrangle is caused by the Line of Head mounting towards the Line of Heart, it's a sign of irresolution and timidity.

Crosses in the Quadrangle show the influences of others on the life of the subject. Those that fall downwards from the Heart Line are influences engendered by the opposite sex; those that rise up may be the result of friendship or love.

The Triangle: This is found in the center of the palm of the hand, below the Quadrangle. It's formed by the lines of Head, Life and Health. If there is no Health Line in the hand, the Line of Fortune will take its place (if that, too, is missing, then use the Fate Line).

When the Triangle is well traced, wide, and the lines are of good color, it will show good health, long life, and a strong intellect. When it is very large, it indicates audacity, generosity, and a noble character. When small and badly formed, it's a sign of meanness, avarice, and lack of intelligence.

First Angle: Formed by the conjunction of the lines of Life and Head. If it is narrow, well made, and acute, it will show a good disposition, sensitivity, delicacy, and wit. If very obtuse, stupidity. If the lines do not actually join, great self-confidence. If the angle is formed down low, right on the Plain of Mars, it's a sign of a very unhappy life.

Second Angle: Formed by the conjunction of the lines of Life and Health (or sometimes Health and Fate). If this angle is well formed, it will show good health; but if it is too sharp, it's a sign of a bad constitution. If it is too heavy and broad, it indicates idleness and an ill nature.

Third Angle: Formed by the conjunction of the lines of Head and Health. If it is well formed and broad, it shows long life and much intelligence. If it is too sharp, a nervous temper. If badly formed, irritability often accompanied by headaches. If very obtuse, it is a sign of stupidity.

The Bracelets (*Rascettes*)

These are the lines which encircle the wrist. However, it's only those placed close to the hand that are important.

The Bracelets show length of life—each line being said to foretell some thirty years of existence—also health, wealth and happiness.

A single line, well made, uncrossed and deep, shows a happy, if short, existence with a calm disposition. The greater the number of lines, if equally well made, the greater the promise of good fortune and happiness.

A Bracelet of four lines is called a "Royal Bracelet," and signifies that the possessor will gain all that this world has to give.

If the lines are chained, it indicates a laborious life. If they are much broken and badly marked, it indicates trouble, distress, and with other bad signs, even disgrace.

A cross on the Bracelets is the sign of a legacy or unexpected gain. An angle promises an inheritance of some sort and an honored old age. Branches are also signs of distinction.

Lines rising from the Bracelets onto the Mount of Luna show long travels. If they end in a star on the mount, it is a warning of danger on one or more of those journeys. If the star shows up in both hands, it indicates death by drowning.

The "Marriage" Lines

These are found passing horizontally across the Mount of Mercury from the percussion of the hand towards the palm.

The long lines only should be considered. They are not necessarily marriages per se, but great loves. Oftimes lines from the Heart Line will be found rising towards the Marriage Lines.

Stars

Stars are generally fatalities, circumstances, or events over which the subject has no personal control. They are formed by three or four lines crossing one another at a central point.

On the Mount of Jupiter: High honor and fortune.

On the Mount of Saturn: Danger of sudden or violent death.

On the Mount of Apollo: Riches and unhappiness; with a good Line of Fortune, celebrity by chance and not long lasting.

On the Mount of Mercury: Danger of theft or dishonor. In a good and talented hand, it is said to be the sign of a successful author.

On the Mount of Mars: Danger of assassination or death in battle.

On the Mount of Luna: Danger of drowning or sign of illness.

On the Mount of Venus: Trouble caused by love or marriage. If close to the Life Line, lawsuits.

On the Line of Fortune: A catastrophe.

On the Plain of Mars: Honor and military glory.

Squares

A square is generally a good sign and gives force and energy to whichever mount or finger it may be found on. The one exception seems to be when it is found on the Mount of Venus. Then it foretells imprisonment, a convent, or other seclusion from the world.

On the lines, it shows preservation from accident.

Triangles

A triangle is a favorable sign. It often indicates an aptitude for scientific pursuits.

On the Mount of Jupiter: Successful diplomacy.

On the Mount of Saturn: Love of the occult sciences, hypnotism, mysticism, superstition.

On the Mount of Apollo: Success in art or literature, scientific art, architecture, sculpture.

On the Mount of Mercury: Success in politics, or in a learned profession.

On the Mount of Mars: Military glory.

On the Mount of Luna: Reason and intuition.

On the Mount of Venus: Prudence in love, calculation in marriage.

Circles

Circles are good signs on the mounts, signifying success and glory, especially on the Mount of Apollo. But on the lines they are bad, showing misfortune. On the Line of Life, they are the sign of loss of sight.

Summary

I think it can be broadly stated that the lines of the left hand show what was intended in your life; "What you were born with," as the *Rom* say. Those of the right hand show what you have made of yourself (the reverse seems to be true with left-handed people). The outline of the hand is hereditary, and it is impossible to alter it to any great degree. But the lines show the habits you encourage; the character you become.

When about to read the hands of a subject, take their left hand in your own and, holding it palm downwards, look carefully at the outline. You will then be able to judge the class of hand—long or short, pointed, spatulate, or square, with or without knots, shape of nails, etc. Then turn the hand over and press the palm so as to tell the hardness or the softness of the hand, as energy or laziness is the keynote of character and modifies all other signs. Then do the same with the right hand.

It is a good idea, especially when first starting, to keep a file of the hands you read. This can be done by using a finger-print kit. Rather than just inking the tips of the fingers, use a rubber roller and ink the entire hand, then press it down firmly on a sheet of clean white paper. As an alternative, sometimes a really good impression can be obtained by simply laying the hand flat on the glass plate of a photocopier or other duplicating machine. In this way, also, it is possible to read palms at a distance by having the client send such an impression to you through the mail. But remember to have them send you a good impression of *both hands*.

• ∽ •

4

Tea Leaf Reading

Interpreting, or "reading," the patterns of tea leaves left in a cup is another very popular Romani method of divination. It was a big favorite in the thirties, forties, and later, when all manner of "Gypsy Tearooms" sprang up, frequently featuring very dubious "Gypsies."

A true Romani will make a complete ritual out of the reading, first making a pot of tea (*meski*) and pouring a full cup for the client. Whilst the client is drinking the tea, the *Rom* is carefully studying him or her and getting initial impressions (I will talk more about this process of cold reading in Chapter 15). Some people, of course, do not like tea and do not want to drink it. At the very least, the client should drink three swallows of the tea. The reader can then pour off most of the excess. Most *Rom* feel it is better if no milk or sugar is added—that it is "pure."

The tea most often used is Chinese tea, but any *large-leafed* variety will do, such as Ceylon or even mint tea (you can also read fine-leafed tea, or even coffee grounds, but they don't seem to form such interesting patterns). Incidentally, if you can't get loose tea, or don't want to make a whole pot, you can simply break open a teabag and tip the contents into the cup, then pour in the hot water.

The cup you use should be a round one, white or very pale colored, with a handle. However elaborate it may be on the outside, it should have no decoration on the inside. This should be completely smooth, with no grooves or the like that could influence the distribution of the tea leaves.

When the tea has been all but entirely drunk (leave about a tablespoonful of liquid), ask the client to take hold of the handle and rotate the cup three times, using the left hand. Most *Rom* say that the cup should be turned counterclockwise. But some say that if the person is female, it should be turned counterclockwise, but if male, then clockwise. As the cup is being rotated, the client should swirl the liquid around the cup, spreading the leaves around, including up towards the rim. The client should finish by tipping the cup upside down on the saucer. I find it helps to have a napkin on the saucer to absorb the spilled tea and leave you with a clean-rimmed cup for the reading.

Finally, the client is to turn the upturned cup around on the saucer and make a wish. In this instance, it doesn't matter in which direction it's turned, or which hand is used; it is up to the whim of the client. Let the cup then drain for a moment or two.

Interpretation

Don't hurry the reading at all. Before saying anything, take all the time you need to look over the cup carefully and study the tea leaves. Turn the cup every way to look at the patterns from every angle. It sometimes happens that you can see two or more shapes or symbols in one cluster of tea leaves—one from one angle and another from a different angle. Always go with your first impression on a symbol. You may later see another symbol but don't forget that first one.

When you begin your actual reading, start from the top of the cup and read downwards. *The handle represents the client.* Those symbols closest to the handle, therefore, will have the greatest influence on the person; those towards the far side of the cup will have only passing influence. Those on the left are generally (though not always) negative influences, and those on the right, positive. Time is judged according to the positioning of the symbol, top to bottom, in the cup. At or near the upper rim is the present. The further down into the cup you go, the further into the future is the influence. So as your reading progresses downward, you are talking about further and further into the future. The bottom of the cup is about a year into the future. The tea leaves are not too accurate after that.

The way certain symbols face can also have meaning. Facing the handle (client), there is a direct effect; facing away, an indirect effect.

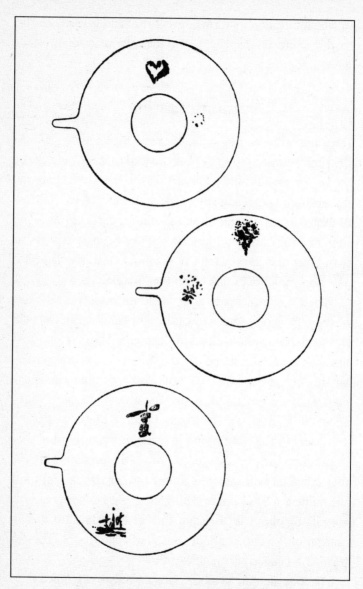

Examples of tea leaf patterns/symbols.

Don't expect all the symbols to look exactly like the things they represent. You will have to use your imagination a great deal. You will find that there is usually just a *suggestion* of, say, a bird or a rabbit or whatever. These suggestions are enough to trigger your mind into seeing them. You'll find this especially true after a little practice. Sometimes the symbols are very distinct, yes, but more often they are not. As with so many forms of divination, the *Rom* use the tea leaves simply as a focal point for their own psychic powers. This is what you will be doing. In the same way, your interpretation of what you see is best coming from within you, rather than just from reading or remembering a long list of symbol meanings (I'll mention this again when we discuss card reading in Chapter 6). I will, however, give you a list of the "traditional" meanings of the symbols, if only as a starting point and as examples of symbol interpretation.

Lines, straight or serpentine, generally indicate roadways, directions; a course to be taken. *Broken lines* are uncertainty or broken promises. *Circles* are completion. *Triangles, horseshoes, bells* and *crowns* frequently mean good luck. *Numbers* are important, indicating hours, days, weeks, etc.; they should be given special attention.

Do notice if two or more symbols seem to tie-in with another. This is especially so where numbers appear; the number being relevant to whatever symbol it is close to.

Before listing the various symbols and their meanings, I would like to share with you an old Gypsy method for answering one of the most frequently asked questions (this was done to me by my grandmother and proved absolutely correct). Many young people—both male and female—want to know when they will get married. Take a teaspoon and balance it on the edge of the cup. Then carefully drip tea into the spoon, a drop at a time (not easy to do but it can be done with practice). After a number of drops, the balance will be broken and the spoon will topple into the cup. The number of drops it takes to upset it is the number of years the client has to wait before marriage.

Tea Leaf Symbols and their Meanings

A

Ace: The Ace of any card suit is of great significance. It indicates that powerful forces are in play. If the Ace is of the Hearts suit, it will deal with domestic and social affairs; the Diamonds suit: financial affairs; Clubs: business, especially contracts and lawsuits; Spades: sorrow, hindrances, upsets.

Acorn: Near the handle of the cup, it indicates coming riches; towards the far side, possible financial help through a second party.

Age: Symbols suggesting an old man or woman indicate a breakdown in your affairs and declining fortune. All your efforts are needed just to keep going.

Airplane: Swift journey. Also, a rise in life (promotion or similar) due to personal effort. A biplane suggests that the success will be due to your association with another person (in partnership or marriage).

Alligator: Great care is needed to avoid injury from others trying to harm you.

Alps: High mountains are indicative of high ideals. Whether or not there is success will depend on what other symbols are attendant. Look also for bars or crosses nearby, or straight, clear lines. Also for numbers, to get an indication of the length of time for the success to come about.

Anchor: Settling down and starting roots. Establishing yourself.

Angel: Good news on its way.

Animal: See the specific animal name. Animals usually indicate action and ability to achieve in one direction or another. But each animal has its own meaning, for instance, a dog for fidelity, a cat for caution, etc.

Ankle: With foot facing away from client, it shows ability misdirected, ambition without understanding, and instability of purpose. Facing client, it shows soundness of judgment, deep understanding, power of direction, and control.

Ant: Symbol of industry, perseverance, and thrift. Success in life through your own efforts.

Anvil: Financial gains will follow some difficulties, but it will involve quite a bit of work on your part.

Arc: Segment of a circle. Indicates an unfinished project or even career. Premature retirement; possible accident.

Arrow: Bad news to come. Probably a disagreeable letter will be received. If there are dots around it, it may be connected with money. *Note:* The direction in which it is pointing may be significant (direction from which news will come?)

Asterisk: There is reason for immediate attention in some direction. Check the nearby symbols. This is something that should never be overlooked.

Axe: Danger and difficulties lie ahead. Possible separation and estrangement. A loss of friends. You will be cut off from your present surroundings. A double-headed axe means a choice, neither possibility being good.

B

Baby: Beginning of a new enterprise. Interestingly enough, Gypsies usually associate this with trouble(s); could be the start of new troubles!

Bag: This is a warning of secret enemies, plans, schemes, plots against you. The fuller the bag appears, the worse will be the condition.

Bagpipes: Discord and disaffection in the family situation. Difficulties in business. Excitement and high tension will tend to bring on ill health and nervousness.

Ball: You will be the plaything of fortune, encountering various ups and downs over which you will seem to have no control.

Balloon: Whether the toy balloon type or the hot air balloon, it indicates a rise in fortunes; a much needed lift.

Basket: If seen near a house, indicates an addition to the family. It can also mean a gift, or that a legacy is coming. A basket of flowers indicates good things ahead.

Bat: False friends. Immediate need for caution. Prepare for the worst, just in case!

Bear: Beware of running into danger through your own stupidity. You may have to overcome obstacles through sheer brute force.

Bed: If the Reader senses that the bed is untidy, it indicates a state of mind that will produce poor results in the client's life and fortunes. If it seems well kept and tidy, then the fortunes will be good and life assured.

Bee: This is a really good symbol, either by itself or in combination with other symbols. It denotes prosperity as the result of industry; the acquisition of fortune; gaining wealth through trade. A general change of fortune for the good.

Bell: Much depends on what is near this symbol; basically, it signifies a coming announcement. By itself, it indicates an announcement which will affect your fortunes. Near the handle, it is especially fortunate. Two bells signify a marriage. Upside down, it is bad news coming.

Bench: Stability of position. No change in circumstances, for the present.

Besom (Broom): Any possible scandal or misrepresentation will be swept away. You are in a position to clean up your "act," your life, your job.

Bird: A bringer of good news. Check other symbols nearby. For example, a bird with a nest means good news concerning the home.

Boat: A possible journey, or a visitor expected from far away.

Book: An open book signifies some sort of revelation to your benefit. A closed book implies need for research, with possible trouble and expense.

Boomerang: Retributive justice. You are about to gather the fruits of your own actions, which may be good or bad.

Boot: If clear and well-formed, this is a protection from danger. If rough and tattered, it indicates disgrace and loss of position.

Bottle: This concerns your health. You may need to check with a doctor.

Bow: This is a good sign, usually tied-in with hope. It also shows the ability to grow. With an arrow, it is the symbol of instant success.

Bracelet: A possible wedding or other union (could be a business partnership).

Branch: With leaves, it is a sign of birth, whether children, the birth of an idea, a new venture, or whatever. Without leaves, it is disappointment; barren ambitions.

Bride: A symbol of sorrow! Possible troubles coming.

Bridge: A way out of difficulties. A path over your problems.

Broom: See *Besom*.

Buffalo: Danger through hazardous speculation. Exercise care and forethought.

Bull: A symbol of gain and prosperity. Shows resourcefulness in business affairs and often shows that very successful financial dealings are about to take place.

Butterfly: Frivolity; vanity. Advise caution. If surrounded by dots, it indicates extravagance with trouble to follow.

Cabbage: Usually indicates jealousy and spite. If squares are near, it can lead to disgrace.

Cage: A symbol of marriage. If the cage is complete and clear of all other symbols, it is a marriage proposal coming.

Cake: Pleasure; celebration. If a ring is near, it can be a wedding or anniversary approaching.

Camel: Progress. Often symbolizes powers of perception which can lead to a better position in life.

Candle: Symbol of a doer of good deeds; a philanthropist. You are likely to be of help to others and, through that, to better yourself.

Canoe: A variation on the Boat—either a visitor coming to you from far away, or *you* will be visiting someone far away.

Carriage: Benefits coming from others. Your path in life will be greatly helped through close friends or acquaintances.

Cart: You are about to gain in some way (probably financially) through some transaction already in hand. Trade will be plentiful and profitable. Your burdens will be light.

Cask or **Barrel:** Empty dreams and vain ambitions. You may have to serve when you'd rather be master.

Castle: A prediction of high office; a good reputation and much power in your sphere of activity. You will have the favor of those in a higher office than yours.

Cat: This is the symbol of a crafty nature. Be on your guard. In business, beware of cheating and fraud. However, if the cat is in a resting position, this is the symbol of domestic comfort. It is also good to have the symbol close to the handle.

Chair: A position of trust and affluence; satisfaction and success. It can also indicate a change of estate and a new occupation.

Chicken: Competence; completion; nervous energy.

Child: Progress and success through the use of natural powers. It is usually a very auspicious sign. Fresh enterprises and new projects will add to your prosperity.

Chimney: Yours will be a position of distinction through service. You may expect changes in your environment.

Church: Formality; ceremonial. Possibly some connection with birth, marriage, or death. You will be associated with others of like ambition.

Cigar: You have dreams of independence and luxury, but be careful that your best projects don't end up in smoke.

Cigarette: You play when you should work and indulge in trifles when there are serious matters at hand.

Circle: This is the perfect form and, by compliance with the natural order of things, you will achieve your end and bring your work to perfection.

Claw: Hurt and injury of a material nature by the actions of rivals and enemies. Financial loss; scandal; hurt to reputation.

Clock: Be attentive—"time flies and waits for no one." Be aware that time is short. This symbol can also mean (a) that there will be speedy recovery from sickness; or (b) news of a death will be forthcoming.

Clouds: You will be going through a dark period but have hope. You will need courage but all should turn out well.

Clover: Luck. If four-leafed, great luck and fortune.

Clown: A symbol of frivolity and inconsequence. Take yourself more seriously.

Coffin: This does not necessarily mean death. It can be the end of a plan, a phase of life, a job, etc. It can, however, indicate failure in business or a long and serious illness.

Coin: Gain and prosperity. Financial aid.

Column: Distinction and honors. You will be placed in some unique position; a position of responsibility. You will be admired.

Comet: An unexpected visitor or unexpected news.

Cone (Pine Cone): Success; achievement. Fertility.

Corn: A symbol of plenty and domestic prosperity.

Cornucopia: A symbol of plenty; freedom from want.

Cow: A peaceful and happy existence with freedom from want. You may be called upon to make some payment; subscription; donation.

Cradle: New projects and fresh enterprises. If the cradle is broken, it indicates trouble coming.

Crocodile: See *Alligator*.

Cross: Light; nucleus of energy. A source for ideas, inspiration. An opportunity will be presenting itself.

Crown: Ascendancy over all difficulties and elevation to a high position. What you have in hand will lead to great success.

Cup: An offering. You may have to make a sacrifice, but it could lead to advancement.

D

Daffodil: Happiness; plans fulfilled.

Dagger: A warning. Be on the watch for people working against you.

Daisy: Usually associated with the spring, this is a symbol of happiness and/or young love.

Dead Man/Woman: Unexpected changes of a radical nature. A dead man indicates these changes associated with a need for more alertness and intelligence; a dead woman indicates these changes associated with affections.

Death: This can be indicated in various ways, a skull or a black flag, for example. This is not necessarily death in the literal sense, however. It can be death of an idea, of a job, of specific plans, of a relationship...as such it can also indicate a new beginning and opportunities for the future. As with Dead Man/Woman (above) it means unexpected changes.

Deer: Good news from the countryside or from a distance. Often this will entail having to make some quick decision.

Demon/Devil: A sign of danger. Look out for false friends and advisers.

Dice: Possible losses through gambling.

Dog: A symbol of friendship. You can rely on the advice and assistance of close friends. If the dog is lying down, you can look forward to a period of peace and tranquility. If the dog seems to be leaping about, it is a sign of joyful news.

Door: Opportunity awaits.

Dot: A dot or point always emphasizes the meaning and importance of the symbol it is close to.

Dragon: New beginnings ahead. Opportunities, but they will only come after some challenges.

Drum: Publicity, which may not be for your own good. It can also symbolize riots and disturbances. Sometimes it indicates domestic disturbances.

Duck: Good news.

Dumbbell: Hard work for little profit. Rivalry and opposition.

Dwarf: Disappointment and failure, with impending trouble.

E

Eagle: A very fortunate sign indicating that aspirations will meet with tremendous success. You will attain to a much higher position than that to which you were born.

Ear: Beware of scandal.

Egg: Beneficial changes and new projects. Success probable in all things. Sometimes indicates an addition to a family.

Elephant: Strength and wisdom. Success after some delay.

Envelope: Unexpected news.

Equestrian: A rider on horseback indicates victory and conquest. Great success.

Explosion: Impending disaster. Violent upsets, disturbances.

Eye: A symbol of intelligence. Be careful in all business dealings.

Eyeglasses: Be extra careful in all business dealings.

F

Face: Can be good or bad depending on the face (take note of which way the face is looking; towards the handle or away from it). A sinister face obviously indicates troubles; a pleasant face, good things. A pleasant face that is a full face (rather than profile) indicates that you will be making a discovery. More than one (pleasant) face shows new friendships.

Fan: False friends. Flirtation. Indiscretion.

Feather: Inconstancy; levity. Take a more serious view of your actions.

Fence: Obstacles and limitations. Difficulties to overcome.

Fencer: Strife and arguments. Avoid litigation or your fortunes will suffer.

File: Disagreement and bickering.

Fir Cone/Fir Tree: Prosperity and success in inspirational types of work.

Fire: Surprising news and hasty action. Guard your word and actions or some trouble may follow.

Fish: One of the most fortunate symbols. It shows increase and prosperity in all affairs; affluence and many profitable interests. Surrounded by dots, it means increase achieved through speculation. If wavy lines are near it, then the good fortune may fluctuate.

Fist: Guard against impulses.

Flag: Often a danger sign, frequently associated with duty. It can also be an opportunity for service and promotion. Possibly special honors.

Flower(s): A single flower shows a favor granted. A bunch of flowers is a sign of many benefits and some honors. Often festivity and celebration.

Fly: Approaching annoyances. Usually connected with domestic problems. Can be an indication of scandal. When several tea leaves take the form of a swarm of flies, it indicates a number of minor annoyances.

Foot: Understanding. You have the power of direction over your affairs. **Two Feet:** You can move in any direction you wish.

Fork: A dilemma arising out of circumstances which you have no power to control. Many annoyances and small worries to come.

Fountain: Great success and happiness.

Fox: Be on your guard. Possible treachery.

Frog: False outlook and wrong ideas. Pride will not carry you far.

Fruit: Always a good sign, showing increase and profit.

Funeral: Failure and disappointment. Look around…usually there are signs of change, and possibly a journey, near this symbol.

G

Gallows: Extreme danger of financial or social failure. Weigh every action and impulse.

Garland: See *Flower(s)*.

Gate: If open, opportunities; closed, a barrier or a challenge.

Ghost: Threat of danger from unexpected sources.

Girl: Happiness, prosperity.

Glass: Symbol of honesty but also fragility. You have nothing to regret except, perhaps, your lack of firmness.

Goat: Misfortune through being obstinate.

Grapes: Increase and prosperity but with accompanying burdens to be carried.

Grasshopper: News coming from a distant friend.

Grave: News of a death.

Guard: You have powerful friends who will stand by you.

Guitar: Happiness in love. Pleasant surroundings.

Gun: Need for unusual care. Possibility of hurt from a distance. If a heart is nearby, this symbolizes a rival in love.

H

Halo: A halo over a figure means special honors coming to the client.

Hammer: Stress and strain. Persistence is called for.

Hand: Friendship, assistance, if extended towards the client (handle). Loss of opportunity if away from client.

Handcuffs: Restraint, restrictions. Difficulties, frustrations.

Hare: Timidity. More than usual bravery needed. A need to be assertive.

Harp: Harmony and concord. A sign of domestic harmony and social success. In a romantic situation, it indicates a happy union. If there are thick lines nearby, it shows there has been a quarrel but all will soon be reconciled.

Hat: A new occupation. Fresh projects, new ambitions and challenges.

Hatchet: See *Axe*.

Hawk: Danger from predatory people. Be on your guard against fraud.

Head: See *Face*.

Heart: Happiness. Affections will be well placed. Possible engagement in marriage. Close friendship. If a crown is near, it denotes honors. If dots are near, financial gain. Two hearts together, marriage and/or a very strong love affair. Look for any initials nearby.

Helmet: Protection. A position of trust.

Hen: A productive mind that will bring a position of honor, so long as you take care not to be defrauded.

Hill: The higher the hill, the better your fortunes. A symbol of attainment.

Hive: Symbol of a home. If there is a swarm of bees, it is a symbol of great success.

Horn: Glad tidings, good fortune. (See also *Cornucopia*).

Horse: Close friendships. A horse's head indicates a lover coming. A horse at full gallop is good news from someone you love dearly.

Horseshoe: Universal symbol of good luck, usually brought about by apparent chance.

Hourglass: You must act quickly, time is running out. Be watchful over those near and dear to you.

House: Safety, possession. A contented life.

I

Insect: Troubles and vexations. Small irritations.

Ivy: A sign of loyal friends.

J

Javelin: See *Spear*.

Jester: See *Clown*.

Jug: A symbol of influential friendships and general well-being. You will be of use to others and, in so doing, benefit yourself. You will have a lot of good friends.

K

Kangaroo: Unexpected travel plans.

Kettle: Domestic happiness.

Key: There are important decisions to be made. You may be entering upon a new path. Carefully consider all new proposals made to you at this time. If you use your opportunities with intelligence, you could unlock the doors to great prosperity and happiness.

Kite: Unusual ambitions. It is within your power to reach great heights. If the kite is without a tail, however, it is the sign of vain ambitions and projects that may end badly.

Knife: Beware of people out to harm you. With the blade pointed towards the handle, it indicates false friends. With the hilt towards the handle, it indicates that you are in command but need to take precautions and be alert. Crossed knives indicate arguments.

L

Ladder: Opportunities for advancement. If dots are near, opportunities for making money.

Lamb: Changes coming about. New ideas, innovations coming into being.

Lamp: Things previously hidden will be revealed. Lost property will be recovered.

Lantern: See *Lamp*.

Leaf: News; letters; messages. Many leaves signify good news, happiness, and success.

Leg: This is a sign of strength and fortitude, also of progress. Note the direction in which the leg is facing.

Letter: As might be assumed, a letter means news is coming, though it could be good or bad. Look for other symbols nearby. For example, a letter with a heart nearby would mean a love letter, or news from a loved one; with a dollar sign nearby it would mean financial news, etc. A letter of the alphabet is an initial for someone's name. Again, see what other symbols are nearby.

Lighthouse: Exercise caution, there is trouble ahead.

Lines: Lines show direction, journeys, progress. The most favorable lines are straight and unbroken. Double lines are roads. Broken lines are uncertainty and broken promises.

Lion: Supremacy. Your position will improve. Your leadership will be recognized.

Loaf of Bread: Your "daily bread." Much depends on what is near. It could mean happiness, increase, well-being or it could mean unhappiness, sickness, loss.

Lock: An obstacle to your progress. A difficult problem that needs to be solved.

ℳ

Man: A visitor. If the figure is facing the handle, the visitor will be staying for a period. If facing away from the handle, he will only be there briefly.

Medal: A sign of distinction and honor. An award for work done. Success in an undertaking, with recognition of that success.

Mermaid: Strength will be needed to resist temptation.

Monk: A symbol for deception and subterfuge. Be very cautious. Some unpleasant incident connected with a man of position or influence will tend to hurt your prospects.

Monkey: Danger from flattery. Be on your guard.

Moon: Possible romantic attachment. New ideas. Start of new undertakings.

Mountains: Great ambitions together with challenges. You will attain great heights, but not without much effort.

Mouse: Poverty. Neglected opportunities. Possibility of burglary.

Mushroom: Advancement through expansion and growth. Can also mean danger to a house in the country.

N

Nail: This symbol denotes malice and cruelty which may be directed against you. Your feelings are going to be hurt.

Necklace: If complete, a conquest and many admirers. If broken, danger of losing the love of one you adore.

Number/Numeral: Any number has significance for the symbol(s) it is near. It could be symbolizing time—hours, days, weeks, etc.—or it could be indicating an amount such as money, or the days of the week themselves. Numbers in themselves do have significance, however. Briefly they are as follows:

One: The number of the Sun. Happiness, success, dignity and honors.

Two: The number of the Moon. Relativity. The dualism of life. The relationship of opposites.

Three: Mars. The three parts of time: past, present, and future. If badly placed, can mean accident, fire, quarrels. If in the clear, resolution.

Four: Mercury. The number of reality and concretion.

Five: Jupiter. Joy, good fortune, good harvest. Increase and propagation.

Six: Venus. The number of cooperation. Harmony, peace, satisfaction. Also pleasures and entertainment.

Seven: Saturn. The number of completion. It indicates wisdom, balance, rest, and perfection.

Eight: Uranus. Dissolution, separation. In the clear it denotes inspiration, genius, and invention.

Nine: Neptune. Can be exile but also pertains to spiritual perception.

Nurse: Illness, though not necessarily for the client.

Oval: See *Egg*.

Owl: A sinister omen. If about to go into a new venture, the client will probably fail. Indicative of trouble and loss in business unless great precaution is taken.

Ox: A sign of prosperity and the friendship of persons in high position.

Pagoda: A sign of traveling in distinguished company.

Palm Tree: After a career of hard work, you will be in a position to retire to the home of your choice. You only have to take advantage of opportunities presented in order to succeed.

Parachute: You will escape from some great danger. You aim high and run the risk of falling, but you will always land on your feet.

Peacock: Luxury; splendor; elegance. A life of luxury. If there is a ring nearby, it denotes a wealthy marriage.

Pig: Good luck. You will not want for food. However, there is a danger of excess through self-indulgence.

Pillar: A symbol of strength and support.

Pillory: See *Stocks*.

Pipe: Take time to contemplate and review your position in life. A break, for replanning and regrouping, is necessary.

Pistol: Danger. Possible disaster. Exercise caution. (Also see *Gun*.)

Pony: See *Horse*.

Pumpkin: The symbol for a warm-hearted person; some-one with a good nature. A diplomat, capable of appealing to others' finer feelings.

Puppy: A frivolous and insincere nature. Inability to focus on any one thing at a time. Indecision.

Pyramid: This symbolizes a great secret that will be revealed. This may be a secret that has held you back in some way. Its revelation will enable you to move forward rapidly. It is, basically, a sign of coming good fortune.

Quiver: A quiver of arrows symbolizes power of command. The ability to lead. You have a message to deliver and will deliver it, come what may.

Question Mark: The unknown. There will be frustrations and many questions that will be unanswered. You need to search for those answers.

R

Rabbit: A sign of timidity. A need to be more assertive. You hesitate too much before making decisions.

Racquet: (As used in tennis, racquetball, etc.) A contest to come. Possibility of trouble and arguments. If the handle of the racquet is towards the cup handle, you will come out on top. If away from it, you will lose.

Rainbow: A sign of hope and encouragement.

Rake: A careful and industrious nature. A tendency to pay attention to the small details.

Rat: Losses through enemies. Be cautious.

Raven, Rook, or **Crow:** You have a roving nature. Your life tends to be shiftless and could easily include illegal activities. You tend to horde things—of your own and of others!

Revolver: See *Gun*.

Ring: This is always a sign of goodwill and friendship which can lead to important events in your life. It can, and often does, tie in with marriage—look for other symbols, and especially initials, nearby. It can also symbolize the completion of a project.

Rose: See *Flower(s)*. The rose can also have a connection with a possible marriage.

§

Saddle: You possess the faculties that will equip you for traveling and exploration. You will soon be sent on a journey.

Saw: Hard work.

Scaffold: The possibility of a law action against you. You will need the best defense you can find.

Scales: Judgment at hand. If the scales are tipped, note which way they go. If they are "heavy" towards the cup handle, judgment will be in your favor.

Scissors: Misunderstandings; confusion; people working at cross-purposes. Possible separation.

Scorpion: A sign of danger. Be very careful, especially in your business dealings.

Shark: Someone of a predatory nature. Note its proximity to the handle.

Sheep: See *Lamb*.

Ship: Success. Good fortune. Your efforts are finally being justly rewarded.

Shoe: A messenger is on the way, with good news.

Skeleton: Possibility of sickness and want. Lean times are coming. You will have to depend on the friendship of others.

Skull: Anger. Be very careful in all dealings with other people.

Sleigh: Rapid progress. Little opposition to your plans.

Snake: Danger from an enemy. Be especially cautious in business. If the snake has its head away from the handle, then you will be the eventual winner.

Soldier: Fighting; arguments; opposition.

Spade: Steady work ahead. Work hard and you will be justly rewarded.

Spear: Wounding, either physically or from scandal.

Spider: Cunning, possible ensnarement. If you use cunning and caution, you can become very rich.

Spiral: Your progress will seem slow and tedious, but you are slowly but surely working your way to the top.

Spoon: An energetic nature, forever striving. You are not afraid to "stir things up" if you think it will help your cause.

Square: Limitation. Sometimes of sinister meaning.
Be cautious.

Star: Good fortune. Opportunities for advancement. A special occasion about to be announced.

Steeple: High aspirations. Ambition.

Stocks or **Pillory:** Restraint. Frustration through being unable to take action.

Submarine: Hidden enemies. Proceed with special caution.

Sun: Fortune. Great happiness. Success.

Swan: A lover. Good luck in love. Notice if there is an initial nearby.

Sword: A menace or a protection—notice which way it is pointing. Pointing towards the handle, it is a threat or menace. Pointing away, it is protection.

T

Table: You are going to be called to a reunion of some sort. A gathering of friends.

Teapot: Consultations; committee meetings.

Tents: Danger of coming troubles. A warning to be on your guard.

Torch: The symbol for a progressive and pioneer-type of character. It denotes a calling; a leader in some movement.

Tortoises or **Turtle:** Slow advancement with much hard work. Little to show for your efforts immediately, though you will reap the reward eventually.

Train: Change. Possible travel.

Tree: A wish will be fulfilled. An oak tree denotes protection and security.

Triangle: Always a good sign. Good luck; success in new enterprises.

Trident: Authority. Possible promotion. Position of respect.

Umbrella: If open, protection from trouble. If closed, frustration in seeking protection.

Vase: A sign of service, by you, to friends.

Violin: A reclusive and independent person. Someone who spends much of their time in study and contemplation. Very much the individualist.

Volcano: A passionate person, frequently with an explosive temper. Violence; sudden passion.

Vulture: Cruelty and oppression. Possibility of theft.

Walking Stick or **Cane:** A friend will be visiting you.

Web: Listen to the advice of friends or you could get tangled up in a situation that would be difficult to get out of.

Whale: You are about to undertake a considerable piece of work, which will eventually reward you well, though not for two to three years.

Wheel: Progress. Also indicates a need for patience, insofar as "if you wait long enough the wheel will eventually turn full circle."

Wig: A sign of deception and false information.

Windmill: Grandiose plans will bring big rewards.

Wings: News coming. Could be good or bad.

Wishbone: Inheritance.

Witch: Wisdom; sage advice.

Wolf: Intrigue. Great cleverness.

Woman: A visitor bearing good news. Look for other symbols nearby for an indication of the type of news.

ʊ

Yacht: See *Ship*.

Yoke: A position of submission, of service. Hard work for someone else.

⚡

Zebra: Special distinction. You are sought out as a friend.

Zodiac: You will often see the symbols for the signs of the zodiac. You can read them according to the interpretations given in the many books on astrology; the effect on the subject being construed by the nearness of the sign to the cup handle. In addition (or as an alternate way of reading them) you can use the very quick overview of the signs' meanings as follows:

Aries: Impulsive changes; excitement. Progress.

Taurus: A sign of money, wealth.

Gemini: A letter. Possibly a short journey.

Cancer: The home. If a ship or arrow is near, it indicates a long journey.

Leo: Pleasures. Children. Sports.

Virgo: Domestic affairs. The accessories of daily life.

Libra: Marriage. Contracts.

Scorpio: Loss. Personal danger. Secret enemies.

Sagittarius: Long voyages. Messages from abroad.

Capricorn: Realization of ambitions. Wishes granted.

Aquarius: Friendship. Social gathering.

Pisces: Restraint. Voluntary seclusion. Confinement.

For any other symbols you may see, which I have not listed here, simply use your intuition. Indeed, if your intuition tells you—strongly—something different from what I have listed above, *go with that intuition*. As with all divination, the symbols seen and used are simply focal points for your own psychic feelings.

• ∾ •

5

Crystal
Gazing

One popular conception of the Gypsy fortune teller is a figure sitting at a table, gazing into a crystal ball. The truth is that although many Gypsies (especially the *Shuvanis*) can see things in the crystal, they cannot necessarily do so on demand, at the whim of the paying client. This is one facet of divination that does call for a certain amount of preparation (both physical and mental) and cannot be done on an around-the-clock basis. For this reason, many Romani *Dukkerers* don't even bother to do it properly most of the time. They simply sit with the ball in front of them, and then go by their own intuition in reading the client. Or as a last resort, if nothing seems to be coming to them, they do what is known as a "cold reading" (I will talk more about cold readings in Chapter 15).

The majority of people do have the ability to see into a crystal ball. As with so many things, it's simply a question of practice. To start, you should work in a room where you will be undisturbed and that is perfectly quiet. You do not want to be distracted in any way, initially, so make sure you are alone and that no one is going to come into the room unexpectedly. Sit in a good, straight-backed chair that is comfortable. Have the crystal ball on a table at a comfortable height in front of you.

Any good reflective surface will do for your gazing: a crystal, a magnifying lens, a highly polished dark-colored surface, a glass of water…yes, a glass of water! Take a regular tumbler (*clear* glass, not decorated) and fill it almost to the brim with water. It will work well. Whatever you use, stand it on a black background, such as a piece of black velvet. This is so that as you gaze at the object, you will not be distracted by anything around it.

Initially, you should have very little light in the room. Later you will be able to do this anywhere, but to start with, try to have everything in your favor. I would suggest just a single candle, which should be placed behind you so that you do not see it directly reflected in the crystal. I would further suggest that you burn some incense. I do find that this helps to induce the right feelings, the right atmosphere. It does actually affect the vibrations of the area. Any good, pleasant-smelling incense will do (e.g., frankincense or sandalwood). Gypsies burn a lot of incense.

It certainly does seem to give a very special "atmosphere" to the room where the reading is taking place.

Now the only secret—if there is a secret—to crystal gazing is in learning to "gaze." *Don't stare!* Don't try to look into the crystal never once blinking your eyes. All you'll get is eye strain! No. Just relax.

Look into the crystal. When you need to blink, just blink. (Try not to even think about whether or not you are blinking or you'll probably get hung up on it and be concentrating more on blinking, or not blinking, than on anything else! Just relax.)

Breathe deeply, inhaling fully and then exhaling fully. Don't try to picture or imagine anything in the crystal. Just look into it. For the first several times you do this, you will probably experience nothing but disappointment. You may try for a week or two, or three, with no results. But don't give up. Suddenly it will happen. Don't gaze for too long at any one session. I would recommend you do not try for longer than ten—absolute maximum fifteen—minutes at any one time. If nothing has happened, just put away your crystal and try again the next night. Incidentally, *some* people do get results right away, first time out.

What will finally happen is that you will see a picture in the crystal. Now you may have a little preliminary "display" just before this. Most people do. You may get the feeling that the crystal is somehow slowly filling with smoke or clouds (usually white in color). As you gaze into it, you will see the whole ball (or water glass, or whatever) filling with swirling white clouds. Then, almost immediately, the clouds will start to fade away again. As they disperse, you will be left with a picture, just like looking into a small three-dimensional television set. This picture may be either in black-and-white or in full color, though most people seem to see in color. Also, it may be a moving picture or it may be still like a regular photograph. Again, most people see moving images.

What you actually see is frequently symbolic, which would tend to give support to the theory that what you see is actually coming from inside you rather than from any outside source. Interpreting it can be a problem. To give an example, you might see a picture of a squirrel running up a tree and pausing at a fork in the branches before running on up one of the limbs. What does that mean, you wonder? What has that to do with anything? On reflection, it should become obvious. It indicates that the person for whom you are reading will shortly have to face a decision, and that decision will affect the direction of the client's life in the immediate future.

Not everything will be presented in these veiled terms, of course, but do be prepared. Many times, first-time crystal gazers say, "I saw all sorts of things but none of it made the slightest bit of sense!" Well, it does make sense if you just take the time to interpret. It's interesting to compare what is seen in a crystal to what is seen in dreams. There is great similarity between dream interpretation and the interpretation of crystal images.

When starting, you pretty much have to accept just whatever is presented to you, indiscriminately. You can, however, learn to see just what you want to see—most important when doing a reading, on request, for someone else. All you do is meditate for a brief moment before starting to gaze. Meditate on what it is that you want to see—the question that you want answered or the information you need to obtain. This meditation need only take a moment or two, just enough time to deliver the message to your unconscious mind. Then, clear your (conscious) mind of all thoughts, breathe deeply, and gaze into the crystal *now trying to keep your mind blank*. Shortly the crystal will cloud (though not always), then clear, and present the thing you wanted to see. It's as simple as that.

Even when you are getting good information, with images flowing freely and delivering all that you want, don't keep at it for too long. Limit yourself to, say, a half-hour maximum from the time you start to see things. You can always come back later and pick up from where you left off. I would suggest a fifteen-minute break between sessions. And as I said above, when first trying and you are unsuccessful, limit yourself to just ten minutes or so. There is a far greater strain when first getting started.

As you progress and become more practiced and accomplished at crystal gazing, you will be able to change the circumstances in which you do it. You will eventually be able to do your work in full daylight (though some sort of low light *is* best, as with watching television) and with someone sitting opposite you asking questions. Initially, however, try to eliminate all distractions.

A final word on the crystal itself if you are opting to use the real thing: What size should it be? The answer is whatever is most comfortable for you. The problem with using overly large balls is that they invariably have imperfections in them which tend to distract the beginner. My favorite size is about three to four inches in diameter. I prefer to have the ball on a stand, but you may prefer to hold it in the palm of your hand; many people do.

The ball does not have to be of pure lead crystal (as should be obvious from the fact that you can actually gaze into virtually any reflective surface). An amethyst ball can be wonderful, as can rose quartz, obsidian, or any other variety. Quartz, glass, or even a plastic ball can be used. Try to get a ball with as few imperfections as possible; the best is with no imperfections whatsoever. With a glass crystal ball, avoid any with bubbles in them, at least to start with. One of the acrylic plastic balls may be best initially. The only real problem with these is that they scratch very easily, so great care must be taken in their handling.

Once you are accomplished at the art, you'll find that imperfections in the ball don't worry you at all. But, as I said above, when starting out you might as well have everything going for you that you can. In fact, if only from that standpoint, I favor quartz crystal rather than glass or plastic, for a true crystal ball does more than just act as a viewfinder for you. It builds up an energy field around you. It actually emits vibrations, setting up a whole ambience, an atmosphere conducive to scrying, complementing that which is put out by the burning incense. My book *Gypsy Witchcraft and Magic* (Llewellyn, 1998) includes the properties and uses of crystals and stones, as used by the Romanies, and the energy fields that they produce.

Most *Rom* simply regard their crystal balls as tools. Yet the tools of any worker who cares are treated with respect. So with the crystal ball. Keep it wrapped in a piece of black silk when not in use. When you first get it, and then again at every Full Moon, wash it carefully in clear water, dry it, and then expose it to the direct light of the Moon for a half-hour or more. By direct light I do not mean moonlight coming through a window pane...open the window and let the actual rays fall on the crystal. Never expose the crystal to direct sunlight.

• ᔛ •

6

Card Reading

I've mentioned before that people love to see objects being used when having their fortunes told. Frequently they attribute almost "magical" properties to these objects. They stare fixedly into the crystal ball, along with the Seer, hoping to catch a glimpse of all that is there. They lock their gaze onto their own palm as though they had never seen it before, and look desperately for indications of those things they are being told. But especially they love to study the cards, even if they have no idea whatsoever of their interpretation. Tarot cards are popular, not just because of the mystique that has built up around them, but also because most decks have a different picture on each card and therefore go further than most other forms of divination in giving the unknowledgeable Querent some kind of clue as to why the Reader says what he or she does.

The tarot cards came from India, as did the Gypsies themselves. In India today, decks of fortune telling cards called the *atouts*, in many respects similar to the tarot, are used. The earliest known tarot decks date from approximately the same time that the Gypsies started leaving India and spreading across Europe around the tenth century. It would seem to follow, then, that we have the Gypsies to thank for giving us these wonderful divinatory cards. Yet many *Dukkerers* are just as happy using regular playing cards as they are using the tarot. I don't think there is any significance to this. Playing cards developed from the tarot anyway. In this section, then, I will look at the use of both tarot cards (Buckland Gypsy and other decks) and ordinary playing cards.

Buckland Gypsy Fortune Telling Tarot Cards

The tarot deck consists of seventy-eight cards divided into two parts: the Major Arcana (twenty-two cards) and the Minor Arcana (fifty-six cards). The Major Arcana is made up of individual cards each bearing a different scene and set of symbols. The Minor Arcana is further divided into four suits: Wands, Cups, Pentacles, and Swords. Each suit has an Ace through Ten, plus Page, Knight, Queen, and King.

The full deck can be used for reading or just the Major Arcana alone. Over the centuries the Minor Arcana came to be used in games of chance and eventually developed into today's playing cards. The suit of Cups became Hearts, Wands became Clubs, Pentacles became Diamonds, and Swords became Spades. Somewhere along the way the Knight was discarded, leaving Page (now "Jack"), Queen, and King. Although today many a Romani reads the tarot, the majority also read the playing cards—even though there are only the *pips* (suit symbols), with no full scenes to interpret.

Over the past two hundred years or so—especially when tarot decks were not easy to find—some Romani families designed their own Major Arcana cards, plus a "Knight" card, to make up the equivalent of a full tarot deck. These new Major Arcana cards frequently bore no resemblance to those of the regular tarot, and even varied greatly from one Gypsy family to the next.

One such Romani deck is that of the Buckland family of Gypsies. The court cards of the Minor Arcana have, in this deck, become Gypsy Kings and Queens. I remember these being used by my grandmother and, I believe, a great aunt had a similar set. In recent years, I asked my mother (now ninety-eight years of age) what had become of the deck. She said she believed it was buried with my grandmother.

Rather than the terms "Major Arcana" and "Minor Arcana," the Gypsies use their own words: *Boro Lil* ("Big Book") and *Tarno Lil* ("Little Book").

As with the tarot, the Buckland Gypsy tarot cards should be read according to the feelings of the Reader. But, as a start, here are some of the more common divinatory meanings given by Buckland Gypsies.

Major Arcana (*Boro Lil*) Divinatory Meanings

1. **Approaching Vardo (*Yek*):** News and/or visitors. Advancement. Plans are coming to fruition. Expect the unexpected. Adventure.

2. **Passing Vardo (*Dui*):** Stability; little change. Opportunity. Hidden secrets. Voyage/journey; change of place.

3. **Departing Vardo (*Trin*):** Missed opportunity. Loss; departure. Need to review, to regroup. Endings.

4. **Flat-Cart (*Stor*):** Swift advance. Agility; maneuverability. Light load. Extroversion. Bright prospects. Caution (don't get too carried away).

5. **Harness (*Panch*):** Restriction; outside control. Little flexibility. Guidance from elsewhere (physical or spiritual).

6. **Neglected Vardo (*Shov*):** Discouragement. Delays. Plans go awry. Frustration. Sickness. Disgrace. Economy. Frugality.

7. **Burning Vardo (*Efta*):** Endings. New beginnings: opportunities. Joy through sorrow. Destruction. Resurrection/ rebirth.

8. ***Koshtermengro* (Making Clothespins) (*Teigh*):** Dexterity. Satisfaction. Patience. Concentration. Rewards to come.

9. **Labor (*Enin*):** Hard work. Servitude. Duties to be performed. Despair. Possible injustice.

10. **Pulling (*Desh*):** Hard work with little reward. Need assistance. Slow but steady progress. Introversion. Monotony.

11. **Double-Horse Team (*Desh ta Yek*):** Assistance. Companionship. Easing of burden(s). Energy; action. Reserve strength.

12. **Money (*Desh ta Dui*):** Rewards. Inheritance. Unexpected wealth/good fortune. Responsibility. Ideas, invention(s).

13. **Poaching (*Desh ta Trin*):** Need for caution. Opportunities need to be grasped. Possible treachery. Hidden enemies. Chance for quick success.

14. **Single Horse (*Desh ta Stor*):** Solitude. Loneliness. Consistency. Monotony. Courage.

15. **Old Man and Girl (*Desh ta Panch*):** Decisions. Changes. Travel. Unexpected companionship. Duty. Diplomacy. Love; attraction.

16. **Bender (*Desh ta Shov*):** Shelter; protection. Brief respite. Opportunity to regroup/rethink. Temporary happiness.

17. ***Kavvi* (Kettle) (*Desh ta Efta*):** Settling in. Comfort. Home. Family. Contentment.

18. **Encampment (*Desh ta Teigh*):** Fruition. Encouragement. Choices/opportunities. Ability to pick and choose. Old friends/new friends. Reinforcement.

19. **Dancers (*Desh ta Enin*):** Celebration. Excitement. Relief. Recognition. Ability.

20. ***Dukkerin'* (Fortune Telling) (*Bish*):** Foreseeing. Psychic abilities. Power; control. Mysteries revealed. Hidden secrets. Initiation. Responsibility.

21. ***Puri Dai/Chuvni* (Wise Woman) (*Bish ta Yek*):** Wisdom. Respect. Good judgment. Skill. Initiative. Inspiration.

22. ***Rodermort* (Significator) (*Bish ta Dui*):** The Seeker.

Major Arcana (*Boro Lil*) Objects and Scenes

Since the Romani cards are relatively unknown to *gaujos* (non-Gypsies), here is a further explanation of some of the objects and scenes depicted in the *Boro Lil*.

Vardo: This is the Romani horse-drawn home, the "wheeled house" as described by Clébert. There are several different types/styles of *vardos*: Bowtop, Ledge, Showman or Burton, Reading, Square-Bow, Thomas, Tong Ledge, and Brush. They are fully furnished with beds, tables, chairs, and even a stove for heating and cooking. The *vardos* are always brightly colored and elaborately decorated. They are pulled by either one or two horses.

Flat-Cart: This is used for fast travel, for carrying things, or for local running about. It can be utilized as a living wagon by adding a canvas "accommodation top," but it is more often a complement to the vardo.

Burning *Vardo*: When a Romani dies, all of his or her possessions are placed inside the *vardo* and it is set on fire. The feeling is that with the ending of the person's life, all things connected with that person should also end, wiping the slate clean. There is also a tie-in with the belief that in destroying the possessions, they will provide for the necessities of the deceased in the afterlife.

Making Clothespins: *Chinnin' the koshters* is the term for making clothespins. Gypsies are very adept at this. They will sometimes spend days doing nothing else. After amassing a pile of them, they will take the clothespins door to door, selling them. It is usual for the men to make the pins and the women to sell them.

Double-Horse Team: When going uphill, or any time the going gets tough, a second horse will be lashed alongside the one pulling the vardo, to give assistance.

Poaching: Gypsies poach out of necessity—the need to get rabbits, fish, fowl in order to eat. Frequently the only place to trap is on the lands of the local Squire. The *Rom* needs to keep a wary eye out for the Squire's Gamekeeper.

Bender: Gypsies make their own tents by taking long sturdy branches and bending them over, sticking both ends into the ground. Hazelnut sticks are best for this. They then throw blankets and tarpaulins over the poles to form a tent.

Kettle: (*Kavvi*) The fire (*yag*), or hearth, is the focal point of any encampment. The kettle is always boiling over it, hanging from its iron hook, the *Kavvisaster*.

Encampment: Frequently many different branches of a Romani family will come together at a campground (the *atchin' tan*)—occasionally different families meet up. There they will renew old acquaintances, make new ones, catch up on news, and pass on information.

Dancers: Gypsies love to dance. The *boshamengro* (fiddler) will strike up, and there is an immediate celebration. However, most Romani dances are done individually, rather than dancing in couples.

Dukkerin': See Chapter 2 for many different forms of Romani *dukkerin'*.

Puri Dai/Chuvni: Every *Rom* family is a matriarchy; at its head is the old grandmother who is the authority figure. She is the "Wise Woman," much in the sense of the Wicca, or Witches, of old. (See my *Buckland's Complete Book of*

Witchcraft, 1986, and also *Gypsy Witchcraft and Magic,* 1998; both from Llewellyn Publications). *Chuvni* is the Romani word for Witch, in that sense.

Significator: This is the card always used to represent the person whose fortune is being told, whether male or female. It is generally placed in the center and the other cards spread around it.

Minor Arcana (*Tarno Lil*) Divinatory Meanings

The cards of the Major Arcana (*Boro Lil*) are not read "reversed"; the whole meaning is found just in the card itself. But with the Minor Arcana (*Tarno Lil*), there *is* a reversed interpretation possible with most of them (the Reader will determine, by feel, whether or not this need be addressed). Twos, fours, tens, court cards, and the entire suit of Diamonds, of course, would appear the same whichever way up the cards are. For these, then, if the Reader wishes to incorporate the reversed meanings, it is suggested he or she make a small mark on each card to indicate whether or not it is upright or reversed.

Hearts

Ace: A love letter, or some other pleasant news.
Reversed: A visit from a friend.

King: A fair, liberal man.
Reversed: A meeting with disappointment.

Queen: A mild, amiable woman.
Reversed: Possibility of having been crossed in love.

Knight: An experienced man with light brown hair and hazel eyes. May be the bearer of messages, good or bad.
Reversed: Caution. Trickery; fraud. Rivalry.

Page: A carefree bachelor (male or female) who thinks only of pleasure.
Reversed: A discontented man or woman, possibly connected with the military.

Ten: Triumph; happiness.
Reversed: Slight anxiety.

Nine: Satisfaction; joy; success.
Reversed: A passing annoyance.

Eight: A fair person's affection.
Reversed: Indifference.

Seven: Pleasant thoughts. Tranquility.
Reversed: Tedium; weariness; boredom.

Six: A sea voyage. Good luck.
Reversed: Sudden change of fortune.

Five: Dreams of great significance.
Reversed: Jealousy.

Four: An engagement to be wed.
Reversed: Difficulty in choosing.

Three: Trust your instincts.
Reversed: Danger of trouble through lack of prudence.

Two: Great success.
Reversed: Exercise caution in business dealings.

Clubs

Ace: Joy, prosperity, or good news.
Reversed: The joy will be of brief duration.

King: A frank, liberal man, fond of serving his friends.
Reversed: He will meet with disappointment.

Queen: An affectionate, quick-witted woman.
Reversed: Jealousy and maliciousness.

Knight: Fair-haired, blue-eyed young man, able to create conflict. Natural leader.
Reversed: Frustration; interruption; discord.

Page: A clever and enterprising young man or woman.
Reversed: A harmless flirt and flatterer.

Ten: Fortune, success, and fame.
Reversed: Need for success.

Nine: A legacy; unexpected gain.
Reversed: A disappointingly small gift received.

Eight: A dark person's affections. If returned, they will result in great prosperity.
Reversed: An unwanted suitor.

Seven: A small debt repaid to you.
Reversed: An even smaller amount received; disappointment.

Six: Hard work resulting in prosperity.
Reversed: Hard work with little or no reward.

Five: Good prospects for the future. A possible wedding.
Reversed: Plans coming to nothing.

Four: A change of fortune; impending evil.
Reversed: Sudden and unexpected bad luck.

Three: Wealthy connections, possibly through marriage.
Reversed: Loss of income.

Two: A disappointment.
Reversed: Opposition to your desires.

Diamonds

Ace: A letter soon to be received.
Reversed: A letter containing bad news.

King: A fair man who can be cunning and dangerous.
Reversed: A very great threat caused by him.

Queen: An ill-bred, scandal-loving woman.
Reversed: She is to be feared.

Knight: Dark, serious person with great patience. Materialistic; methodical.
Reversed: Carelessness; idleness; stagnation.

Page: An unfaithful friend or employee.
Reversed: Many problems caused by him or her.

Ten: A relocation of home or business; a journey.
Reversed: The change, or journey, will not be for the better.

Nine: Delay, with resultant annoyance.
Reversed: A quarrel with your family or lover.

Eight: An attempt to make love.
Reversed: The attempt thwarted.

Seven: Satire; mockery.
Reversed: A foolish scandal.

Six: Unhappy ends to a marriage.
Reversed: Loss of your possessions.

Five: Children bringing joy; prosperity in business.
Reversed: An unexpected financial loss.

Four: Trouble and aggravations.
Reversed: Loss of a friend or good employee.

Three: Disputes and arguments, in the home and office.
Reversed: A lawsuit.

Two: A love affair; a close friendship developing.
Reversed: Scandal. Loss of a friend.

Spades

Ace: An emotional relationship that could cause trouble.
Reversed: Unexpected bad news.

King: The envious man; an enemy or dishonest lawyer who is to be feared.
Reversed: Impotence; malice.

Queen: A widow.
Reversed: A dangerous and malicious woman.

Knight: Bravery and skill. Good defender. Strength; dominance.
Reversed: Extravagance; conceit; boastfulness. Inability to act.

Page: A dark, ill-bred young man or woman.
Reversed: He or she is plotting against you.

Ten: Grief; prison; restraint.
Reversed: Brief affliction.

Nine: News of a death.
Reversed: The death of a near relative.

Eight: Approaching illness.
Reversed: A broken marriage/engagement. An offer refused.

Seven: Many annoyances.
Reversed: Foolish intrigue.

Six: Good plans and intentions meeting with failure.
Reversed: Lack of ideas and plans.

Five: Quarreling brought about by short tempers.
Reversed: Bickering; petty annoyances.

Four: Being passed over for promotion. Missed opportunities.
Reversed: Jealousy and envy.

Three: Faithlessness in love. Bitterness.
Reversed: News of indiscretions.

Two: Separation. Change.
Reversed: Unwanted and unexpected change.

Any picture (court) card between two others of equal value (e.g., a Queen between two sevens) indicates that the person represented by that picture card (as a Significator) runs the risk of being caught up in a conflict.

Pairs, Triplets and Quartettes

When two, three, or four cards of the same denomination come together they have special meaning:

Aces

Four Aces: Danger; failure in business; sometimes imprisonment.
If one or more of them is reversed: The danger is lessened.

Three Aces: Good tidings.
One or more reversed: Folly.

Two Aces: A plot.
Reversed: It is unsuccessful.

Kings

Four Kings: Rewards; dignities; honors.
Reversed: These will be less but will be received sooner.

Three Kings: A consultation on important business, with very satisfactory results.
Reversed: Doubtful success.

Two Kings: A partnership in business.
Reversed: A partnership dissolved.

Queen

Four Queens: Company; society.
Reversed: Things will not go well.

Three Queens: Friendly calls.
Reversed: Scandal and deceit; gossip.

Two Queens: A meeting between friends.
Reversed: Trouble, in which one will involve the other.

Knights

Four Knights: Brotherhood (Sisterhood); camaraderie. An important meeting.
Reversed: Plans fall apart.

Three Knights: Consultation. Opinions sought. Ability to make decisions.
Reversed: Ridicule; object of humor; loss of face.

Two Knights: Object of infatuation. Time for reflection.
Reversed: Rivalry; petty jealousies.

Pages

Four Pages: A noisy party, mostly young people.
Reversed: A drinking bout.

Three Pages: False friends.
Reversed: A quarrel with someone beneath you.

Two Pages: Evil intentions.
Reversed: Danger.

Tens

Four Tens: Great success in plans.
Reversed: The success won't be so great, but it will be sure.

Three Tens: Improper conduct.
Reversed: Failure.

Two Tens: Change of profession.
Reversed: This is only a distant possibility.

Nines

Four Nines: A great surprise.
Reversed: A celebration.

Three Nines: Joy; fortune; good health.
Reversed: Wealth lost by imprudence.

Two Nines: A small gain.
Reversed: Small losses through gambling.

Eights

Four Eights: A short journey.
Reversed: The return of a friend or relative.

Three Eights: Thoughts of marriage.
Reversed: Flirtation; foolishness.

Two Eights: A brief dream of love.
Reversed: Small pleasure and minor pain.

Sevens

Four Sevens: Intrigue among low people. Threats, snares, and disputes.
Reversed: The harm will fall back on the perpetrators.

Three Sevens: Sickness; premature old age.
Reversed: Slight and brief indisposition.

Two Sevens: Levity.
Reversed: Regret.

Significator

Major Arcana (*Boro Lil*) card number twenty-two is the one always used to represent the person whose cards you are reading. That card is set down in the middle. On top of it place something belonging to the Querent to make a contact. It used to be that a Romani Reader would start out by saying, "Cross my palm with silver," and the Querent would give a coin. This was not so much to get paid for the reading as to make a contact—establishing a link between Reader and Querent. Personally, I keep a pile of old English pennies beside me. I ask the Querent to take one and hold it between his or her palms for a few moments, concentrating their energies into it. Then I take the coin and hold it myself, absorbing those energies, before laying it down on top of the center card.

The remaining seventy-seven cards are handed to the Querent to shuffle. If the Querent has any particular question that needs answering, he or she should concentrate on that question while shuffling the cards.

Once shuffled, the Querent should cut the deck to the left, with the left hand, into three piles. The Reader now gathers them up (picking up the center pile first) into one deck and lays them out for reading.

Layouts

No one layout seems more popular than others with the Gypsies. They use whatever seems to work best for them. As with the cards themselves, many use layouts that have been passed down through the family and may not be found anywhere else. The layouts given can be used just as effectively with any tarot deck. (Alternate instructions are given when they differ from use with the Buckland Gypsy deck.)

Buckland Seven Star

This is a layout my grandmother would use a lot. Although I have never found it anywhere else, I am including it here both for her sake and because I think it's a very good layout! It uses only the twenty-two cards of the Major Arcana (*Boro Lil*). It is good for the immediate future—the next six to twelve months.

Number twenty-two, the Significator, is put down in the center to represent the Querent. The other twenty-one cards are then well shuffled by the Querent and cut as described above. The Reader lays down the cards, face down, in threes, around the center card in the pattern shown (see illustration). There are two ways of reading from this layout:

1. The Querent indicates one card only in the first pile. This the Reader turns over and interprets. The Querent then indicates one card only in the second pile and so on.

2. The Reader turns over all three cards in each pile, in turn, and reads from the one or two (seldom all three) that particularly strike him or her. The positions in the layout are as follows:

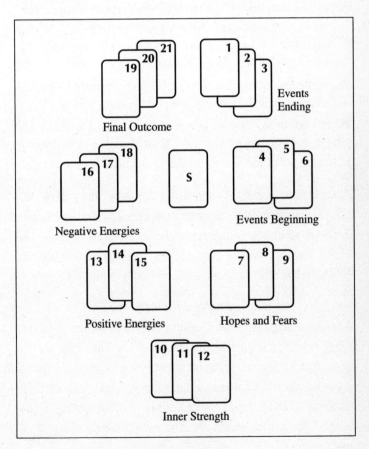

Buckland Seven Star

Events Ending: A brief look at what has led up to the present and is just finishing.

Events Beginning: Those forces now coming into play. What is shaping up.

Hopes and Fears: Of the Querent.

Inner Strength: The reserve the Querent is able to draw upon in times of need.

Positive Energies: Those energies available—from close friends, family, events, situations, etc.—that may be called upon if needed (sometimes those actual people/ events can be seen in the cards).

Negative Energies: Those energies that may inadvertently be drawn in from other people, situations, events.

Final Outcome: Overall result of the forces at work in this time period. *Note:* This is the final outcome of this particular set of forces, not of the Querent's life in general.

Alternate instructions: When using any other tarot deck, the Fool is always used to represent the client as the Significator in this layout. My grandmother never referred to it as "The Fool," however, but as "The Seeker," and she always seemed able to relate the card to the individual in some way.

Lucky Thirteen

After shuffling, have the Querent cut the full deck into two piles, with the left hand, placing it to the left. Take up the right-hand pile and count off thirteen cards from the top of it (if this should be a very small pile with less than thirteen cards in it, have the Querent shuffle and cut again). These are the cards from which the reading will be done.

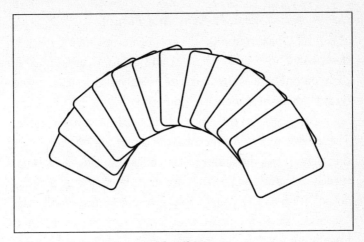

Lucky Thirteen

Fan out the cards into a half circle. Interpret any doubles, triples, or quartettes, and then read the cards in threes as follows: after reading the first three, let the third card become the first card of the next three. Read those and again let the third card of that set become the first of the next three and so on. This will give you six sets of threes in all.

This is a general reading covering general events with, perhaps, a look at the present situation also. If the Querent had been concentrating on any particular questions whilst shuffling, the answer will be obvious in the cards. If for any reason it is not answered—or if the Querent has another important question related to the previous one—then you may draw the card from the top of the left-hand pile, and that will hold the answer. However, this card should not be drawn unless absolutely necessary.

Past, Present, and Future

Have the Querent shuffle the full deck and then cut it, as described above. Take the top and bottom cards and lay them on one side as the "Surprise." Deal out three cards, side by side, then three more on top of those. Continue until you have thirty cards in three piles, left to right, ten in each pile. The left pile represents the Past; the center pile—the Present; the right pile—the Future. The piles are, one at a time, turned over and spread. They are interpreted, giving particular attention to any pairs, triplets, or quartettes. Finally, the "Surprise" cards are turned over. They represent unexpected forces—for good or ill—that may come into play at any time.

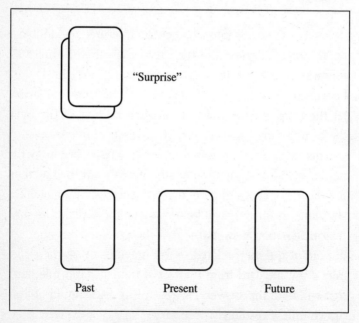

Past, Present, and Future

Sevens

This layout uses a modified deck of the Minor Arcana only (a total of thirty-two cards), where everything below the sevens is dropped out. Place the Significator on the table. From the top of the shuffled and cut deck, count through six cards and place the seventh face up on the table below the Significator. Count through six more cards and lay the seventh to the right of the first one. Count through six more and lay down the seventh. Again, count through six and lay down the seventh. Now take the remaining cards, mix with the discarded ones, and have the Querent shuffle and cut again. Continue with this: count off six and lay down the seventh, continuing until you have a total of eleven cards on the table in a line below the Significator (see illustration below).

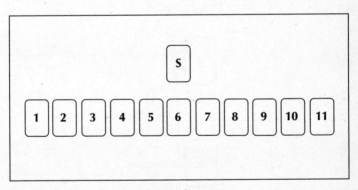

Sevens (layout)

Interpret the meanings of any pairs, triplets, or quartettes. Then count from the left of the line to the seventh card and place this, above and to the left of, the Significator (see illustration on page 98). This seventh card represents the forces that have been working on the Querent in the past. Take the card on the far left of the line and the card on the far right and pull them down below the line, side by side. These represent the Querent's hopes (left) and fears (right). Again, count seven cards from the left along the remaining original line. Place this seventh card down below the bottom two. This is a person whose influence will be coming into the Querent's life in the near future, for good or ill. You now have seven cards left in the original line. Take the middle three of these and place them at the bottom. The four left in the original line are the forces now working all around the client. The bottom three are indicative of what the final outcome will be.

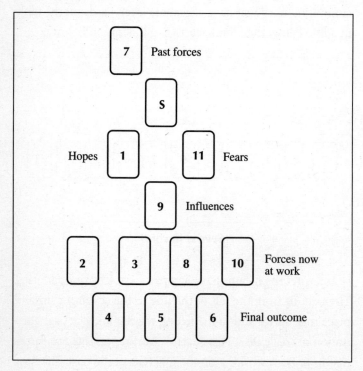

Sevens (interpretation)

The Star

For this layout, the Querent chooses twenty-four cards. They are laid out around the Significator, in the form of a star. Going in a counterclockwise direction, lay the first eight cards face down and equally spaced around the center Significator (start in the top center position and finish at the top right). Then lay the next eight on top of these and the final eight on top of those.

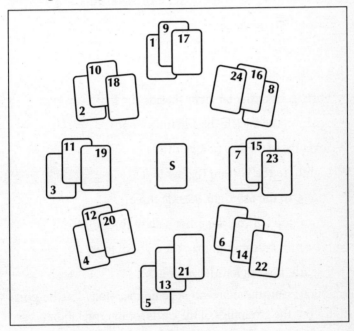

The Star

Start the reading by turning over the first set of three cards (top center). Proceed again in a counterclockwise direction.

Reading from this layout, the positions of the cards do not carry any specific meaning. The cards are read almost like a narrative, a story, going straight from one pile to the next around the Significator.

The Council

[It is of passing interest, perhaps, that this layout involves thirteen cards—the number traditionally found in a Wiccan coven—and is called "The Council"…of Elders?]

Twelve cards are picked by the Querent. The Significator is placed, face up, in the center of the table. The twelve are laid down as follows:

- First card is placed to the right of the Significator.

- Second, to the left.

- Third, goes above it.

- Fourth, below.

- Fifth, goes to the far right (beside the first).

- Sixth, to the far left (beside the second).

- Seventh, to the top (above three).

- Eighth, to the bottom (below four).

- Ninth, to the top right (beside three).

- Tenth, top left (on the other side of three).

- Eleventh, bottom right (to the right of four).

- Twelfth, bottom left (left of four).

Once again there are no specific meanings for the positions, but the groupings of the cards for interpretation is very interesting. Number Seven, at the top, is read first. Then the full horizontal line below it: Ten, Three and Nine. Then Six, followed by the full vertical line of Ten, Two and Twelve.

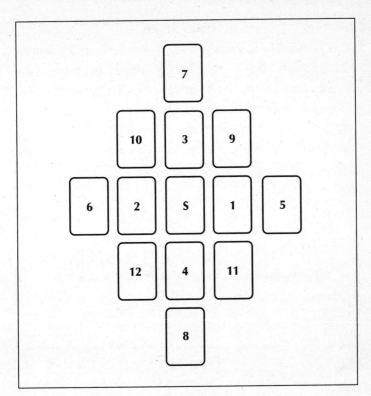

The Council

Next the vertical line of Nine, One and Eleven, followed by Five. Then the horizontal line of Twelve, Four and Eleven. And, finally, Eight. All of these are read according to their proximity to the Significator.

It may sound somewhat complicated, but reference to the illustration will show that it is actually fairly straightforward.

Gypsy Seven

This is useful for a quick reading. Seven cards are chosen by the Querent. They are laid out in a line to the right of the Significator. The meanings are as follows: One—inner self; Two—forces at work around Querent; Three—past influences; Four—hopes and dreams; Five—family and friends; Six—forces opposing; Seven—final outcome.

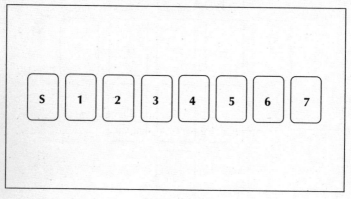

Gypsy Seven

Keltic Cross

This is probably the most popular layout in tarot card reading, and is used by quite a number of *Rom.* Ten cards are picked, and with the Significator, are laid out according to the illustration.

- First card covers the Significator ("What covers him"—i.e., the outward appearance that the Querent presents).

- Second crosses the first ("What crosses him"—forces working against the Querent).

- Third goes above ("What crowns him"—the Querent's ideals).

- Fourth, below ("Beneath him"—the real Querent, deep down inside).
- Fifth, to the right ("Behind him"—the past).
- Sixth, to the left ("In front of him"—the immediate future).

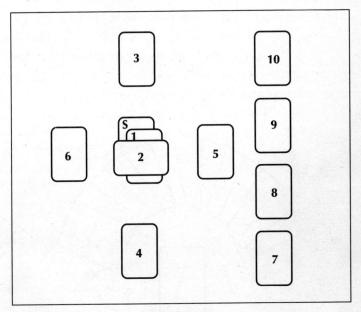

Keltic Cross

The remaining four go in a vertical line to the right of this cross, being placed from the bottom up to the top:

- Seventh ("His house"—his close friends and family).
- Eighth ("Himself"—the overall person), often a synthesis of the Significator and cards One, Three and Four.
- Ninth ("His hopes and fears"), sometimes reflecting Two.
- Tenth ("The final outcome").

The Fan

Thirteen cards are drawn for this layout. They are spread, face down, in the shape of a fan, above the Significator. The cards are read in groups of five; the fifth card becoming the first card of the next group each time. This gives three groupings. The first group represents the past. The second group—the present. And the third group—the future. The middle (third) card of each group is then drawn out and they are placed together. They are now read in relation to one another to give a general reading or summary.

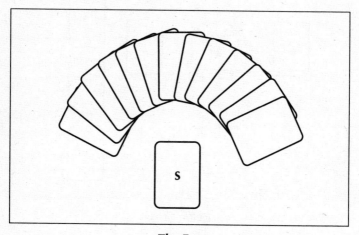

The Fan

Other Tarot Cards

Today there are over two thousand different decks of tarot cards on the market. Which of these you choose to use is your preference. The *Rom* don't seem to have any general consensus on this. I have seen many, most of them handed on down through the Gypsy family. Some of them, as mentioned, are even made by the Gypsies themselves, based on the traditional designs. My personal favorites are the Morgan-Greer deck, the Hanson-Roberts deck, the Crowley Thoth deck, and a Royal Fez Moroccan deck that I have colored myself, to give it my own *mana.** So, it's up to you. I suggest you try several decks and see which one you most enjoy working with.

Significator and Cards

As has been show, the method of working with cards is for the client to choose a certain number of the cards and for the Reader to lay out those cards in a special order, each position being given a particular meaning. The Reader then interprets them, reading both from the individual card and from its position and relationship to the other cards.

Usually one card is chosen, at the outset, to represent the Querent in the reading (Significator). The favored Romani method of choosing the Significator is for the Reader to go through all the cards in the tarot deck and pick out one card that she feels is most representative of the Querent. This she determines simply from "feelings." If you happen to know,

---

* "The supernaturally powerful charge of dynamic energy inherent in… sacred objects…." (*Putnam's Concise Mythological Dictionary*, Joseph Kaster, Capricorn Books, 1964)

very well, the person for whom you are reading then it is usually fairly easy to find a card that seems to be just right. But if you are reading for a stranger, you need to somehow "tune in" and then connect up with one particular card.

The Gypsy way of "tuning in" is through psychometry (touching or being near an object belonging to a client). "Cross my palm with silver" is a familiar Gypsy greeting before fortune telling. Yet this is not just a way to get payment for the reading. When passing across the "piece of silver" (or dollar bill, or whatever), the Querent is giving the Reader something which he or she has handled, something which will make a connection between the two of them. From this the Gypsy can then determine—usually with amazing accuracy—which of the seventy-eight tarot cards is the right one to use to represent that person. You may not be proficient at psychometry (it's actually just a question of practice), but you can soon become extremely accurate at picking out the right card. (See my *Buckland's Complete Book of Witchcraft*, Lesson Eight.)

I suggest you start by actually holding the Querent's hands in yours. Close your eyes and meditate for a moment on the person. Keep your mind open and try to get a feeling for the type of person the Querent is. Is he or she happy or unhappy? Carefree or worried? Short-tempered or easygoing? Try to picture the Querent in a home environment, then in a working one. Whether or not you get clear pictures, don't worry too much about it. Release the hands and pick up the cards. Go fairly quickly through the deck until you come to one card that seems to say to you, "Hey! This is it!" And there will be one. If you can't find it, go quickly through all the cards a second time.

When I do this, I go through till I find the one card, but then I keep on going. Usually I get to the end of the deck and am certain that the one I picked was right. But sometimes, as I continue, I find one or two more that seem equally suitable! If so, I place the two or three cards together in a line and once again take my client's hands. Just holding the hands and looking at the now-narrowed choices, I find, directs me to one particular card much more strongly than the others.

But supposing no matter how hard you try, you just can't get any feeling; you just can't find the "right" card to represent your client. Then (as a last resort) give the deck to the client to pick out the one which he or she feels is most representative of themselves.

Many books on the tarot state that you have very few choices for the Querent's card. They say that if, for example, your client is an older, dark-haired woman then you should use the Queen of Swords as her card...nonsense! Everyone is an individual, and so everyone will be represented by a different card.

Once you have selected the Significator, put it to one side and give the Querent the rest of the deck to shuffle. As the Querent shuffles, ask him or her to concentrate on any questions or problems they may have. Then the Querent must cut the cards, with the left hand, into three piles. You turn over those three piles and study, and read, the top cards. You read them as individual cards first, then in combination. This is known as a "general reading" and will give some sort of an idea as to how the main reading is going to go, particularly as it applies to the question the client was concentrating upon.

Next, stack up the cards again and spread them, face down, across the table. Ask the Querent to pick out ten of them (the number the Querent is to pick will actually depend upon the layout you are going to use). These the Querent must place in a pile, one on top of the other, face down, in the order in which he or she draws them. These chosen cards, together with the Significator, are the ones that will be used in the reading. The others may be put to one side.

When laying out the chosen cards, they are always laid face down (with the exception of the Significator, which is kept face up). They should also be laid down in the order in which they were chosen—the first card chosen should be laid down first, the second laid second, and so on. Since the first card the Querent chose is at the bottom of the pile, you can simply lay them down dealing off the bottom. But here is a way I have found more convenient—at least for me. The cards, as chosen by the Querent, are in their pile with the first one picked on the bottom and the others on top, as described above. In other words, in reverse order to the way you want to use them.

Simply take up the pile and count them out, placing the top card on the table, the next one on top of it, the next on that, and so on. What you are doing, then, is reversing the order to bring the first chosen card to the top of the pile. And you are also doing this—counting them out—for the useful purpose of ensuring that the correct number of cards have been picked. Working from there, you can deal off from the top of the pile, laying down that first chosen card in the first position, and so on.

Layouts

For the most popular layouts, refer to pages 92 to 104 for instructions, using any tarot deck of your choice.

Interpretation

For the actual interpretation of the cards, I think I can probably do no better than repeat what I said in my book *Buckland's Complete Book of Witchcraft*:

> How, then, do you interpret? Go by your instincts; your feelings, your intuition. As you turn over each card, think of the position that it occupies. For example (in the Keltic Cross layout): position #6—the Immediate Future. What, of the illustration on the card, strikes you most forcibly as you turn it face up? Invariably one thing—one small part of the overall design—will "hit your eye" first. Think of what that object, color or symbol, can mean in relation to (in this example) the Querent's immediate future. For example, suppose you are using a Rider-Waite deck... and you turn up the "Death" card. Does this mean Death is in the near future? No! The interpretation given in one book is, "transformation; change. Sometimes followed by or preceding destruction. Sometimes birth or renewal." It could mean the death of an idea, or a job—perhaps leading to "rebirth" in a new job (incidentally, I should mention here that it will help immeasurably if you disregard the titles on the Major Arcana cards. "Death" is not necessarily death; "Justice" is not necessarily justice; the "Devil" not necessarily the Devil, and so on).
>
> By going by our method, there are far more possibilities. You might be struck by the small boat in the background and associate it with travel. Or you might be impressed by the sun rising (or setting?) between the two towers on the right; or the rose on the banner; or the bishop-like figure...there are so many things which

might strike you forcibly. You will find it a different thing each time you read the cards, giving a different—and therefore far more personal—reading for each individual. So, don't go by (any book of interpretation)...use your own powers.

I would just add that what you see should be told to the Querent in as easy a narrative style as possible. You don't have to say *why* you say what you say (unless you are specifically asked), and there's no need to mix your words with mystical, esoteric terms to try to impress and make it sound more profound! If you do see "bad news"—possible death or an accident—then choose your words especially carefully. Suggest that the client take special precautions or avoid certain undertakings. After all, don't forget that what you are seeing is only an indication of what is likely to happen if things proceed as they are. But NOTHING HAS TO BE. Anything can be changed, for we do create our own reality.

I have mentioned the four suits of the tarot: Wands, Cups, Pentacles, and Swords. When interpreting the cards, remember that Wands are frequently associated with sexual pursuits and feelings, and also with projects and undertakings. Cups are associated with love and close friendships. Pentacles are often indicative of money, and Swords of troubles and misfortunes.

One last word...at the very beginning, the Querent concentrated on a particular question when first shuffling the cards. That question should have been answered in the course of the reading. When you finish, *ask* if it was answered. If the Querent says, "No," then ask what the question was, and look back over the cards. The answer will be there. It usually comes out naturally, as part of the reading, but sometimes it doesn't so you have to look more specifically.

Regular Playing Cards

As I said above, many *Rom Dukkerers* are quite happy to use regular playing cards (the Minor Arcana) rather than tarot cards. I think this is because they are able to draw on their psychic powers a lot more easily, perhaps, than other people are. They are therefore able to "read" from the plain *pips* on the cards without having to rely on actual pictures present-ed for interpretation. Of course, it isn't hard for anyone to learn the meanings of fifty-two different cards though, as with the tarot, there is a lot more to a good reading than just repeating book-learned equivalents.

As with the start of a tarot reading, while the Querent shuffles the cards, he or she should concentrate on any question or problem that they are particularly concerned about. And, again, that question should be answered during the course of the reading.

After the shuffling you may (if you like—this is not mandatory) have the Querent cut the deck into three piles, so that you can turn them over and give a quick general reading from the top three cards.

If you are doing a reading using only a certain number of cards, then spread the deck, face down, across the table and let the Querent pick that number of cards (as in the tarot instructions previously). If you are using all the cards, sim-ply stack them up and start working with them.

Significator

A card to represent the Querent is not always used when reading from playing cards. When one is used, however, it is one of the court cards: for a man, one of the Kings; for a woman, one of the Queens. For a very young person—male or female—use the Jacks. The particular suit chosen depends upon the client's coloring: white skin—Diamonds; medium fair skin—Hearts; medium dark skin—Clubs; dark skin—Spades.

Layouts

As will be seen, these layouts use the complete Minor Arcana deck. Others use a modified deck of thirty-two cards; that is, a deck with only the Aces, Kings, Queens, Jacks, tens, nines, eights, and sevens. Everything below the sevens is dropped out.

The Nine Square

This layout uses the Minor Arcana deck of fifty-two cards. First, the Significator is removed and put to the side, then the Querent shuffles the deck. The Querent cuts them into two piles with the left hand. Remove the bottom card from each pile and discard it. The Querent rejoins the two piles and again shuffles. You then take the deck and deal out three piles of five cards each. The next card is laid, face down, to one side. This is known as the "Surprise." Now deal off a second row of three piles of five cards, immediately below the first row. Again lay aside the next card, face down, in the Surprise pile. Now lay out a third row below the other two, of five cards to a pile.

This should leave you with just two cards. The top one you place with the others in the Surprise pile. The remaining card you turn face up in front of you. If its suit is Hearts, you pick up piles One, Five, and Nine, and discard the other piles. If the suit is Diamonds, pick piles Three, Five, and Seven. If Clubs, piles Two, Five, and Eight. And if Spades, pick piles Four, Five, and Six.

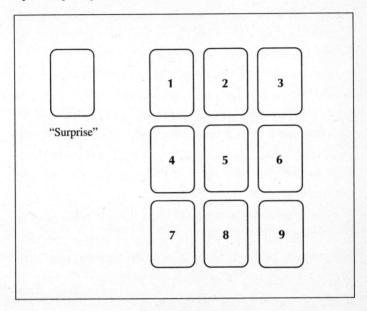

The Nine Square

The Significator is now added to the three piles chosen, and all sixteen of these cards are shuffled by the Querent. Turn them face up and spread them, in a fan, across the table in front of you. These cards are the ones read, paying special attention to their closeness or distance from the Significator. Finally the Surprise cards are turned over. These are indicative of unexpected event(s) that are going to come into play in the near future.

Romani Star

This uses the modified deck of thirty-two cards. First, pick out the Significator, then hand the balance of the deck to the Querent to shuffle. As usual, have the Querent concentrate on any special question that needs to be answered.

Take the deck and count off the top eleven cards. These are discarded. The Querent reshuffles the balance and cuts them into two piles. You take off the top card and the bottom card from each pile and these are placed to one side (separate from the discarded cards). The sixteen cards which now remain are once again shuffled by the Querent and handed to you.

Lay the Significator in the center of the table, then lay out the chosen cards as follows:

• First card, sideways to the right of the Significator.

• Second, sideways to the left.

• Third, vertical, above the Significator.

• Fourth, vertical, below.

• Fifth, vertical, to the right, next to the first.

• Sixth, vertical, to the left, next to the second.

• Seventh, sideways, above the third.

• Eighth, sideways, below the fourth.

• Ninth, sideways, to the right, beside the fifth.

• Tenth, sideways, to the left, beside the sixth.

• Eleventh, vertical, above the seventh.

• Twelfth, vertical, below the eighth.

• Thirteenth, diagonally, in top right quarter (between the third and the first).

- Fourteenth, diagonally, in top left quarter, (between the third and the sixth).
- Fifteenth, diagonally, in lower left quarter (between second and eighth).
- Sixteenth, diagonally, in lower right quarter (between fourth and first).

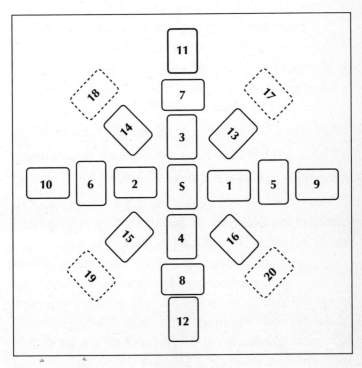

Romani Star

Start reading the cards in pairs, beginning with One and Two, followed by Three and Four. Then Five and Nine; Six and Ten; Seven and Eleven; Eight and Twelve; Thirteen and Fifteen; and Fourteen and Sixteen. The cards closer to the Significator (e.g., One and Two) will, of course, have more effect on the Querent. Those further away (e.g., Six and Ten) will have less effect, though it may be that it is more a question of time, rather than immediate influence. In other words, those close to the Significator will be influencing the Querent in the immediate future; those further away will influence in the far distant future. Only you will be able to tell this from how you feel as you read the cards.

Having read these seventeen cards, take up the four that were set to one side and lay them down as follows:

- The first (I'll actually call it number Seventeen, to continue from the others we have laid down) is laid in the top right, sideways, above number thirteen.

- Eighteen is laid sideways, in the top left, above fourteen.

- Nineteen is laid sideways, in the lower left, below Fifteen.

- Twenty is laid sideways, in the lower right, below Sixteen.

These last four cards are also read in pairs: Seventeen with Nineteen; and Eighteen with Twenty. They represent the final outcome—the end to which all the other cards are leading.

One word on this layout, and on any similar layouts. With the Significator and those cards laid down the same way, vertically, it is obvious when a card is reversed. Even with those on the diagonal you can tell. But with cards laying sideways, you can't immediately tell. All you need do is move slightly (or simply turn your head a little) to the left—as though you were sitting behind card number Ten—and look at the layout from that perspective to study the sideways cards.

Seven Times Two Plus Two

This seems like a long-winded way of saying "Sixteen," but the Gypsies put special significance on the number seven, hence the name Seven Times Two Plus Two.

After having well shuffled the modified deck of thirty-two, deal out into two smaller decks of sixteen cards each. Have the Querent choose one of these decks. Lay aside the top card, as the "Surprise," and then turn up the other fifteen in a half-circle in front of you. If the Significator is not among them, start over, and repeat till it is one of the fifteen.

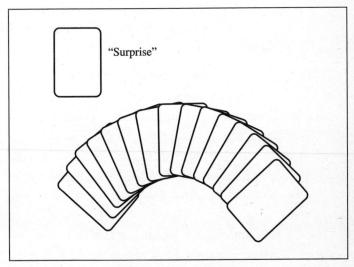

Seven Times Two Plus Two

Now proceed to give a general reading from the cards, first by interpreting the meaning of any pairs, triplets, or quartettes among them; then by counting them in sevens, going from left to right, and reading those two (seventh) cards together; and finally by taking the cards at either extremity of the line and pairing them.

Next, gather up the fifteen cards, have the Querent shuffle and cut them, then deal them into three piles of five cards each. From each of these piles, withdraw the top card and place them on the "Surprise" card you had put to one side. This now gives you four piles of four cards each, side by side on the table. Ask the Querent to choose one of these four piles. Turn it over and spread the cards. This is the set "For Himself." Take the pack furthest to your left and turn this up, below that first one. This is "His House." The third pack is laid out below that—"For Those Who Do Not Expect It" (i.e., unexpected events that are coming up). The fourth pack, laid out now at the bottom, is "The Surprise" (i.e., the final outcome).

The Pyramid

The Querent, after thoroughly shuffling the whole Minor Arcana deck, will hand the cards to you. You will lay down the Significator, face up, as the top card of the pyramid. Beneath it, lay the next two cards from the deck. Beneath them, lay the next three cards. Beneath them, the next four, and so on. Continue putting down cards until you have seven rows.

The top row (the solitary Significator), of course, represents the Querent. The second row represents the influences presently strongest around the Querent. The third row is the powers the Querent can draw upon—friends, influences, etc. The fourth row are those forces working against the Querent. The fifth row shows his or her past. The sixth shows the Querent's hopes, fears, and dreams. And the seventh row indicates the final outcome.

Comment on any pairs, triplets, or quartettes (two, three or four of a kind) that happen to lay side by side (see pages 89 to 91 for interpretation).

Now study the last card laid down in each row (including the Significator). There are seven of them. These cards will give you a general idea of "luck," or good fortune, for the coming month. See which suit appears the most in these seven. If it's Hearts, there will be a lot of luck. If it's Diamonds, quite a bit. Clubs, no more than usual. Spades, noticeable bad luck. Should you find that no one suit has more cards than the others (a tie), turn up more cards (in a separate pile) from the remaining cards, until one suit appears to match one of those tied.

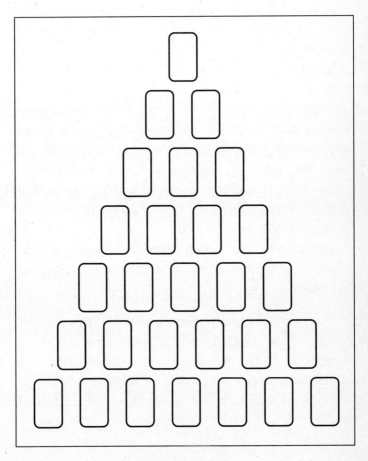

The Pyramid

Cross of the Year

This layout uses the complete Minor Arcana and is used for looking at the year ahead. The cards are arranged in twelve rows moving downwards, representing the twelve months of the year; and columns across (the "arms" of the cross) represent the four seasons.

No Significator is used. The Querent shuffles the deck and then you lay them out in threes, one set below the other, for twelve rows. In line with the sixth and seventh rows, lay two cards (one above the other) to the left; two to the right; two to the left; two to the right; and so on until all cards have been laid down.

As stated, the rows of three in the vertical column represent the months; the first (top) row being January, second row February, and so on. At the "arms" of the cross, the first four cards (two outer columns on the far left of the main vertical) represent Spring, the second four (next to the main vertical) Summer, then the first four on the right Fall, and the last four Winter.

The "months" are read first, then the "seasons" are consulted for additional information affecting the three months in that season.

There are many, many more layouts used by the Gypsies. It's impossible to include them all here; that would need a separate book. The ones I have included here seem to be particular favorites and are found in many areas of the country. Also, many of the layouts for the tarot cards can be used equally well with regular playing cards.

Cross of the Year

Interpretation

Most Gypsies give their own interpretation to the cards depending, of course, on the individual for whom they are reading. However, there does seem to be a lot of agreement on general interpretation (for example, the Ace of Hearts—a love letter; the Ace of Clubs—prosperity). You can use the interpretations given for the Minor Arcana (*Tarno Lil*) of the Buckland Gypsy cards (pages 84–91) including the interpretation of pairs, triplets, and quartettes—two, three, or four cards of the same value—following one another. You will, of course, ignore the Knight of each suit and read the Page as the Jack.

"Rom Rhymes" for Interpretation

Interestingly, some Romanies in the north of England use rhymes to go with the card meanings. I tend to think that these are usually given when the client simply cuts the deck to turn up one card, for a quick fortune. Most of these rhymes seem to be aimed at female clients.

Hearts

Ace   *Your fate is sealed on a Friday night,*
'Midst music, song and pure delight.

King   *A lover true now waits for you.*
Don't say 'No' whate'er you do.

Queen   *The Queen of Hearts, the King of Love,*
A ring, a rose, and a silken glove.

Jack   *Beware of Cupid and his darts!*
Your fate is held by the Knave of Hearts.

Ten   *Triumph in all things near at hand.*
Spread the good word throughout the land.

Nine   *A whisper of love, a whisper of hate,*
Tie a silk thread to the garden gate.

Eight   *A twilight kiss and a dream of bliss—*
A little black dog will lead you to this.

Seven   *On Tuesday you may look to find*
A lover who is true and kind.

Six   *If a blue butterfly you see,*
It is your luck to go over the sea.

Five   *Five this week's your lucky number,*
and fortune comes to you in slumber.

Four   *As you sit in the firelight glow,*
His name is writ in the embers low.

Three   *The third hour of the third day.*
The King of Hearts shall win you away.

Two   *The viper's tongue, the sting of lies,*
Beyond dark clouds are blue, blue skies.

Diamonds

Ace   *A song of love, a kiss that burns,*
And your luck on the Ace of Diamond turns.

King   *When bees in honeysuckle sip,*
Love shall be sealed with a scarlet lip.

Queen   *This week or next will likely bring*
Good luck and an engagement ring.

Jack   *A butterfly wing set in a ring,*
This to you good luck should bring.

Ten   *A change of view, a sense of waste,*
A change of residence in haste.

Nine   *Two days from now, take care what you say,*
'Twill bind you for five years and a day.

Eight   *Should you doubt his love for you,*
Place a golden bead in your left shoe.

Seven   *Three men, three men in love with you.*
The first and last will ne'er be true.

Six   *If you would be a rich man's wife,*
Cut a silken cord with a silver knife.

Five   *If a large black cat you see,*
'Twill bring good luck 'twixt one and three.

Four   *Under your pillow, place a rose.*
For luck to your lover where'er he goes.

Three   *Three words of love in a garden fair—*
He shall be waiting for you there.

Two   *A spider spinning on the wall*
Shows he'll be brave, and strong, and tall.

Clubs

Ace   *Two hearts entwined on the trunk of a tree—*
The man who cut it is true to thee.

King   *A kiss within an hour of noon*
Will bring a wedding very soon.

Queen   *A lover's knot that none shall break,*
Two shall ask, the third shall take.

Jack   *Two eyes of blue and hair like gold,*
And two strong arms about you fold.

Ten   *Wednesday for fortune is the day,*
So be prepared, let fate point the way.

Nine   *Love, wealth and happiness will be yours,*
If every night you lock three doors.

Eight   *Someone is waiting, someone you know,*
You will have luck when you meet in the snow.

Seven   *His words are fair, his heart is black,*
So turn to one whose name is Jack.

Six   *The six of clubs will bring you hope.*
Make three knots in a piece of rope.

Five   *If when the moon is full you kiss,*
It will lead to married bliss.

Four   *A Gypsy woman will tell you the truth—*
You are fated to marry the love of your youth.

Three   *Wealth, good health, and a lover true,*
These are the three in store for you.

Two   *The Priest of Isis scans your fate—*
Your true love waits at the old church gate.

Spades

Ace   *If hearts be true, then naught can stay*
Love's arrow on a coming day.

King   *When Friday dawns a golden morn,*
You'll thank the stars that you were born.

Queen   *A kitten, a kitten as white as snow,*
By her tomorrow your luck you'll know.

Jack   *If his name begins with G,*
You will ever happy be.

Ten   *Ten long days, till set of sun,*
Behind jail bars; you cannot run.

Nine   *For love and luck, when the sun goes down,*
Rub a new penny and change your gown.

Eight   *At ten in the morning on Wednesday,*
You will be traveling far away.

Seven   *Your lucky color is apple green.*
And your lucky number, twice fourteen.

Six   *His heart is gold, his eyes are gray,*
You'll meet him twice on Saturday.

Five   *On a summer's day, by the deep blue sea,*
You'll have luck if you count to fifty-three.

Four   *A letter written in purple ink,*
Will bring you more than you can think.

Three   *Queen of his heart you'll ever reign,*
If you should meet him in a train.

Two   *Though sorrow come with parting pain,*
He shall come back to you again.

• ∽ •

7

Dice

Having studied the most popular forms of *dukkerin'* used by the Romani, let's look now at some of the other methods of telling fortunes. Most of them use very simple, basic tools. A good example is dice. Many a *Rom* will carry a set of dice in his pocket. They are less cumbersome than a deck of cards... and less obvious.

In different parts of England there are variations found in the interpretations given to the dice, but on the whole they seem to follow the same pattern. Basically, the throw of the dice (three of them) gives an answer to your question(s). The answer, or prophesy, is said to come true within nine days. Here is the simplest method of using them.

Mark a chalk circle (or scratch it in the dirt of the ground) about twelve inches in diameter. The three dice should be held in the right hand, by the Querent, who should concentrate on a question. Then, in complete silence, the Querent cups the dice in both hands and gives them a good shake. The Querent then throws the dice into the circle. Any die or dice that roll out of the circle are disregarded. If all of them roll out, this foretells a quarrel or an estrangement, and the Querent must throw again. If all of them roll out a second time, then no fortune can be told that day.

Of those that stay in the circle, add the numbers that show. The meaning of their sum is as follows:

One: Loneliness; loss.

Two: Love or infatuation.

Three: A pleasant surprise is coming.

Four: An unpleasant surprise.

Five: You will meet with a stranger who will have a strong influence on you.

Six: You will lose something you value.

Seven: There will be a scandal involving you.

Eight: A wrong that you did in the past will catch up with you.

Nine: There is a wedding in the near future.

Ten: Business advancement.

Eleven: The death of someone you know.

Twelve: You will soon receive a letter of some importance.

Thirteen: There will be cause for you to weep.

Fourteen: A new admirer.

Fifteen: Be especially cautious, trouble threatens.

Sixteen: A happy journey.

Seventeen: Profitable business is coming to you from across water.

Eighteen: Some very great good is coming to you.

There is a second way of using the dice. This is the method usually used by a fortune teller, or *Dukkerer*, at a fairground ("Three questions answered for $2!"). Just two dice are used and there is a set list of questions. These questions may be written down, but it is far more likely that the *Dukkerer* has them in her head and, whatever question the Querent asks of her, she can apply it to one of the set questions (see pages 130–131). They certainly seem to cover most contingencies.

The two dice are held in the Querent's right hand for a moment while concentrating on a question. The Querent will then state the question out loud (for the benefit of the interpreter—you) and throw the dice down on the table. There is no circle to throw them into, as in the previous example. You simply give the answer according to the upturned faces of the two dice by using the number combination and their sum. (Answers are listed on pages 131–161.)

For example, suppose the Querent asks question seventeen, "Will my secret be discovered?" (see page 130) and then throws a five and a two. The answer for a throw of a five and a two—the sum being seven—is "Nobody even thinks of inquiring about it." (See answer seventeen on page 146.) It can be seen that a large number of questions can be asked and answered in this way.

Questions

1. Does the person I love think of me often?
2. Will anyone soon date me?
3. What must I do to please my love?
4. Shall I answer?
5. Shall I agree to what is asked of me?
6. How many admirers will I have?
7. How many times will I be married?
8. What sort of person will my spouse be?
9. What does he or she think of me?
10. May I trust him or her?
11. Does he or she love me?
12. Does he or she think that I love them?
13. Will my heart remain free much longer?
14. Shall I soon get married?
15. Shall I experience many adventures?
16. Shall I be rich?
17. Will my secret be discovered?
18. Am I thought to be good looking?
19. Am I thought to be discreet, witty, and interesting?
20. Will I marry the person I am thinking of?
21. Shall I do it?
22. Shall I see my love again soon?
23. Shall I soon receive a letter?
24. Which of the two shall I choose?
25. Shall I soon receive a present?
26. Shall I soon make a journey?
27. Will my condition shortly be changed?

28. Will my wish be fulfilled?
29. What is he or she doing at present?
30. What will my spouse be?
31. Will it prove a blessing to me?
32. Shall I soon receive the news I'm waiting for?

Answers

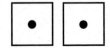

Two

1. They think of you as much as you think of them.
2. Tomorrow morning, about eleven o'clock.
3. Whatever you do, do it gracefully, and especially, always treat them with respect.
4. Yes, but word your reply discreetly.
5. No. You must not.
6. A dozen at least!
7. One.
8. Young, slender, and fair complexioned.
9. That you are a very special person.
10. No, you may not, for they are not good at heart.
11. He or she cannot help themself.
12. You have shown it plainly enough.
13. You know very well that it has not been free this long while!
14. In a week.
15. Your life will be as peaceful as a quiet lake.
16. You will always have all you need.
17. It would be a good thing if it were discovered.

18. All except your nose.
19. Discreet indeed, but not witty, and only interesting at times!
20. No.
21. Why not?
22. Tomorrow.
23. Not as soon as you would wish.
24. The one who has the longest nose.
25. Very soon, and it will be a kiss.
26. Yes. A very long one.
27. Yes, to your joy and happiness.
28. It will.
29. Busy attending to his or her own affairs.
30. Very rich.
31. It will lead to the greatest happiness.
32. Sooner than you expect.

Three

1. Not in the least.
2. Much too soon, as it will turn out.
3. Always dress well. Never have bare arms unless absolutely necessary.
4. It is hazardous.
5. Yes, without the slightest fear.
6. As many admirers as you will have spouses.
7. Twice.

8. Fat and round as a ball, but of a very sweet disposition.

9. That you have stolen their heart.

10. Have you not already had enough proof of this?

11. He or she is yours, heart and soul.

12. He or she has doubts.

13. Tomorrow, when you first go out, you will meet someone who will become very special to you.

14. In two years.

15. Your life will move along like a foaming torrent.

16. As rich as you are at present.

17. No, but it would be good to disclose it as soon as possible.

18. When you are pleasant and friendly, but not when you are ill-tempered.

19. To one person at least, very interesting.

20. If you really want him or her.

21. If you wish; it will do no harm.

22. Within three weeks.

23. Yes, but not the one you had hoped for.

24. The darker one.

25. Yes.

26. You will soon be seeing cities you never expected to see.

27. When you shall wish it changed.

28. If it is really your wish.

29. Looking through books and papers.

30. An engineer.

31. No, that's impossible.

32. Not for quite a while.

Four

1. Always.
2. Aren't you always surrounded by admirers?
3. Treat him or her with frankness and honesty.
4. It would be better if you didn't.
5. Yes, but do it prudently.
6. Five.
7. Once, to a very jealous person.
8. Loving and tender.
9. That you are very hard-hearted.
10. You don't need to mistrust too much.
11. Can't you tell from their face?
12. Hopes so, but has many doubts.
13. At five o'clock tomorrow afternoon, love's arrow will strike!
14. In six weeks.
15. Many thrilling adventures.
16. Quite wealthy.
17. It will, unless you are always on your guard.
18. Quite attractive.
19. Reasonably so.
20. Yes.
21. If it will give you pleasure.
22. No. You are separated forever.
23. There is one on the way right now.
24. The one who always gazes upon you with such a shrewd expression.

25. Yes, but from someone different from the one you thought.

26. A short, sentimental one.

27. Yes, but you won't benefit from it.

28. If you do everything you can to bring it about.

29. Reading a book.

30. Very spiritual.

31. It will bring you both joy and sorrow.

32. Never.

Four

1. Are you not fascinating?

2. Yes, but be careful. It is a rogue who will be next.

3. Show a little more kindness to other human beings.

4. Frankly and without affectation.

5. It would be too cruel to refuse.

6. Only one. But that one will admire you more than all others put together.

7. Once.

8. Very homely, but in your eyes, very handsome.

9. That it would be dangerous to trust you.

10. Oh, yes. With all your heart.

11. Haven't you noticed how he or she blushes when looking at you?

12. Without a doubt.

13. At the next social event you attend, your heart will be touched.

14. Never.
15. Too many by far.
16. You'll have so much wealth you won't know what to do with it.
17. It is discovered already.
18. Not greatly so, but somewhat.
19. Mischievous.
20. Yes, and others.
21. Do what you can't help doing.
22. Very soon.
23. The one you would like to receive, you will never receive.
24. The one with the long hair.
25. Very soon.
26. Yes. One that you are looking forward to.
27. It will depend entirely on yourself.
28. It will. Certainly.
29. Dining with someone else.
30. A lawyer.
31. It will bring you joy and happiness.
32. Perhaps within the year.

 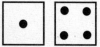

Five

1. They would like to but dare not.
2. When you stop worrying about it.
3. Show your appreciation of their friendship.
4. It would never do to keep silent.

5. You can't do otherwise.

6. Four, possibly five.

7. Once, and it will be the joy of your life. Name begins with a "G."

8. Very tall with a light complexion. Wears spectacles and is very friendly to everyone.

9. That he or she can neither understand your actions nor your words.

10. You can believe what they say and discount the gossip.

11. You can find that out next time you pass him or her a drink. If, in taking it, they touch your hand, then there is love.

12. Yes, and is flattered by it.

13. At the moment your heart is not free. Examine it.

14. Within a year.

15. Very many. Mostly with rogues and robbers.

16. Rich in love and friendship, but not in money.

17. You think that it's a secret, but it never has been one.

18. Passably so.

19. You are thought to be capricious.

20. It's very doubtful.

21. It will do no good, and no harm.

22. If you send an invitation, otherwise no.

23. Very soon, a very tender one.

24. The one who first reaches out to touch you.

25. Yes, a living one.

26. Yes, but not the one you're presently thinking of.

27. Not so very soon.

28. Yes, but not as soon as you'd like.

29. Sleeping.
30. A doctor.
31. Only so long as you keep your heart pure and true.
32. Yes, in a few hours.

Five

1. They are far too busy with other things to keep thinking of you!
2. If you would treat a certain person with a little more regard, they would be happy to do so.
3. Don't pay so much attention to others.
4. Answer as it deserves to be answered.
5. Follow your heart.
6. Many, but most of them you'll find boring.
7. Once, to a very unromantic person whose name begins with a "B."
8. Very tall and of dark complexion, somewhat quarrelsome, jealous, but with the best of intentions.
9. That it would be very dangerous to see you often.
10. Inquire what others say about him or her. There is a lot of truth in what is said.
11. With heart and soul.
12. Since the last time you were together, he or she is sure of it.
13. You know very well that right now you are in love.
14. In five months.
15. No. Very few.

16. You will have money, which is not necessarily the same as being rich.

17. If you tell no one...no.

18. If you could be a little less self-conscious, you would be thought so.

19. Many people think you a genius but, because of that, think you have many faults.

20. Yes, you will.

21. Certainly not!

22. At a time when you least expect it.

23. Yes, and it will make you very happy.

24. The one with the largest hands.

25. Not soon.

26. Yes, the one you are thinking of.

27. Not in the way you wish.

28. Yes, and sooner than you expect.

29. Arguing with someone.

30. Connected with science.

31. Yes, though it won't appear so at first.

32. Within three days...or never.

Six

1. As often as circumstances permit.

2. You will have wrinkles before that happens to you!

3. Don't be so terribly affected. Try to be more natural.

4. Yes, just as your heart prompts you.

5. Be very careful. You might be laughed at.

6. Seven, at least.
7. Once, to a dear, good, and amiable person.
8. Friendly and cheerful, of a romantic turn, somewhat poetical, but just a trifle weak.
9. That you are the guiding star of his or her existence.
10. You can tell by looking into those honest eyes.
11. Only as a brother or sister would.
12. If you keep giving those tender glances, he or she can hardly doubt it.
13. At the moment you love one, but you will soon love another.
14. Within four years.
15. Your life will be a very weary one.
16. If you are careful and watch your money.
17. There is one person who knows it but will not tell it.
18. Some think so...others do not.
19. You are generally thought to be heartless and soulless.
20. You know yourself that is impossible.
21. Think what your family would say.
22. Yes, in the not too far distant future.
23. Yes, but it will bring sad news.
24. The one who blushes most often.
25. You must be patient for a while.
26. Not as soon as you hope.
27. Very soon, and in a particular way.
28. It will be fulfilled, but not completely, and not quite as you had hoped.
29. Spending time with an older person of the opposite sex.

30. A merchant.
31. If you take it as it is meant.
32. Probably within a month.

Six

1. Yes, as well you know.
2. Yes, but they won't be serious about it.
3. Do not be over-sweet.
4. It would be best if you did.
5. Yes, if you can do it without blushing.
6. Two; one dark and one fair.
7. More than once, and none of them good.
8. A small person, full of conceit and vanity.
9. That you are as near perfect as possible.
10. It is well to be prudent.
11. Yes, but he or she also loves many others.
12. Not exactly, but they think it would be easy to win your heart.
13. For a year yet, but no longer.
14. In six years. No sooner, no matter how hard you try.
15. Many, but none especially interesting.
16. You will have plenty of money, but if you or your spouse should gamble, you will lose it all.
17. You will betray yourself.
18. A lot of people think you homely, some few think you pretty, and one or two think you beautiful.

19. You are thought to be quick at repartee but not really witty.

20. Yes, if you succeed in winning his or her heart within two weeks.

21. Do it, even though there is someone it will greatly displease.

22. You will have to wait awhile.

23. Yes, a very long one.

24. The more modest of the two.

25. Very soon, and one which will delight you.

26. Yes, but one that will cost you many tears.

27. Soon, and by an unexpected occurrence.

28. Yes, and more fully than you have reason to expect.

29. Preparing witticisms to speak in your presence.

30. A broker.

31. It will cost you many tears at first, but will end up well.

32. Very soon.

Six

1. Thinking of you now and very tenderly.

2. Quite a number.

3. Work on your hair.

4. Place a poppy under your pillow tonight, and you will dream of what you should do.

5. Ask advice of your closest friend.

6. One older man, who you won't care for.

7. Twice.

8. A person of strong character; high minded and energetic, with wit and humor also.

9. That you have broken many hearts.

10. No one better deserves confidence.

11. He or she is a true friend to you, that is all.

12. They have never thought about it at all.

13. It will always be free enough.

14. Very soon.

15. Many, and most of them interesting.

16. If you keep from speculating.

17. If you can refrain from babbling!

18. If you didn't wrinkle your nose when you laugh, you would be better looking.

19. Some people think you peculiar, but there are a few who really understand you.

20. If you can truly love them.

21. Yes, it will give you great pleasure.

22. Not until you both have gray hairs.

23. Not soon, but when you do it will be a very tender one.

24. The least pretentious one.

25. At the moment no one is thinking of giving you anything.

26. One which will give you much pleasure.

27. Soon, and in a way you would never have dreamed of.

28. Sooner than you expect.

29. Sighing over the low state of his or her finances.

30. A farmer.

31. If you can always stay cheerful and optimistic.

32. You should know when you may expect it.

Seven

1. Yes, and regrets it.
2. Congratulate yourself if they don't, for there are few worth having.
3. Don't get so sentimental, don't talk so much, and try to use a little more common sense.
4. What is spoken vanishes; what is written remains.
5. You may grant all that is asked for nothing unworthy will be requested.
6. Over twenty, five of whom are already in love with you.
7. Three times.
8. A large person in love with themself.
9. That you would like to bring him or her to despair.
10. Consult your best female friend about this.
11. Their heart has long belonged to another and would never be unfaithful.
12. No, but he or she thinks how pleasant it would be if you did.
13. Your heart is free at present but won't be for much longer.
14. Not until you love a certain person more tenderly than you do at present.
15. Yes, and they will prove too exciting for you.
16. So long as you make good use of the money.
17. No, it will not.
18. If you wear more subdued clothing and improve your complexion.

19. Discreet, but very vain and proud.
20. Yes, if they are not already engaged.
21. Of course. You would be a fool not to.
22. Not very soon.
23. Yes, and the paper will be wet with tears.
24. The one with the larger ears.
25. Someone will offer you one, but you would do well to reject it.
26. An important and joyful occurrence will prevent it.
27. Not very soon.
28. That will depend on you. Act prudently.
29. Hurrying to see you.
30. A government worker.
31. If you can keep your presence of mind.
32. Not for some time.

Seven

1. All the time.
2. Yes, but it won't bring you happiness.
3. Just enjoy life; relax and be yourself
4. Without hesitation.
5. Go to your mother for advice.
6. Two. One's initial is "L."
7. Only once.
8. Young and handsome, with rosy cheeks.
9. That you have been deceitful.

10. Yes, but not too far.

11. From the moment you first met.

12. He or she thinks that at least you would like to love them.

13. The next journey you take you will fall in love.

14. Within two years.

15. Some pleasant ones, and kind friends will protect you from unpleasant ones.

16. No, never.

17. Nobody even thinks of inquiring about it.

18. Yes.

19. You are thought to be thoroughly charming.

20. You would, if it were not for a false friend.

21. Certainly. You can't do better.

22. He or she is working on how to bring that about.

23. A very foolish one quite soon.

24. The one with the large mouth.

25. A splendid one, very soon.

26. You will have the opportunity, though you may not take it.

27. Yes, in the way you expect.

28. It will be your own fault if it's not.

29. Practicing what he or she is to say to you.

30. A professional person.

31. It will be the prelude to the fulfillment of your warmest wishes.

32. You will soon receive it and shed tears of joy.

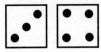

Seven

1. Yes, but not in the way you would like.
2. You will soon have more than you can accept.
3. Get a good suntan.
4. Yes, but make it clear you are not happy about it.
5. Only in part.
6. Many, but few of them attractive.
7. If you accepted all that offered, it would be twenty-five times at least!
8. Tall and thin as a beanpole.
9. "You do not deserve my love."
10. Fully and frankly.
11. Yes, but resists it thinking you do not return the love.
12. Not that you truly love, just that you are a little smitten.
13. It will be a long time before you give away your heart.
14. Within the year.
15. No.
16. Gold will rain down upon you.
17. You had better be on your guard or it will leak out.
18. Don't think about it.
19. Good natured enough but rather vain.
20. If you would flirt less with others, he or she would be a lot more interested in you.
21. People will laugh at you but don't let that stop you.
22. It will only happen by accident.
23. Yes, but you won't understand it.

24. The one who agrees with you.
25. Yes, one with which you will be delighted.
26. A sad occurrence will prevent it.
27. Yes, but not in the way you expect.
28. Wicked people will prevent it.
29. Thinking how boring life can be.
30. A literary person.
31. It will give you initial pleasure but later tears.
32. Yes, and you know who it will be from.

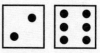

Eight

1. Frequently.
2. Yes, a plain-looking person with a good sense of humor.
3. Pay a little more attention to them.
4. Answer what your heart dictates.
5. No.
6. About a dozen.
7. Once, or possibly not at all.
8. A great favorite, especially of the opposite sex.
9. That you don't like them.
10. Has he or she ever done anything to make you distrust them?
11. With great longing.
12. Did so once but no longer.
13. In about six weeks, by starlight, your heart will be softened.

14. In a year or two.
15. A reasonable number.
16. Labor always to be rich in contentment of mind.
17. It is half discovered already.
18. Absolutely beautiful.
19. In every respect.
20. No, so don't expect to.
21. If you don't, you're lost.
22. In a few weeks.
23. Yes, in eight days.
24. The one who gives you a gift.
25. One which you will soon wish you never got
26. Yes, in the company of someone of the opposite sex.
27. In a very agreeable manner.
28. An unexpected accident will prevent it.
29. Contemplating a change of job/lifestyle.
30. A business person.
31. If you are strong enough to suppress all vanity.
32. Not as soon as you'd like; there will be a wait.

Eight

1. More than you think of them.
2. No one worthy of having.
3. Not eat so heartily.
4. There's no danger in it.
5. If you do, you will bring joy to one heart and break another.

6. Two, both good looking.
7. Once, and that will be one too many.
8. A drunkard and a gambler.
9. "He or she has caused me so much suffering I can never forgive them."
10. Yes, but keep your wits about you.
11. As much as possible, but that may not be much.
12. No. He or she thinks your feelings are those of a brother or sister.
13. Is your heart really your own now?
14. Within three years.
15. Only a few.
16. You will have gold by the bushel.
17. Not if you are discreet.
18. You roll your eyes too much, your ears are not well shaped, but your hands are well formed.
19. More or less so.
20. You don't really wish it.
21. If you are prudent, it can do no harm.
22. By the end of next summer.
23. Not the one you wish. That will be delayed.
24. The one who is polite and well mannered.
25. Yes, over which you will shed tears of joy.
26. Very soon, and in pleasant company.
27. Yes, and exactly to your wishes.
28. It will, and it will bring you great happiness.
29. Counting the hours till seeing you again.
30. A mechanic.
31. Everything is a blessing. Sometimes we misinterpret.
32. Not soon. Don't be impatient.

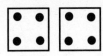

Eight

1. Don't expect too much.

2. The first person you meet tomorrow.

3. Argue with him or her a little, but not too much.

4. Yes, but choose your words carefully.

5. Ask the advice of a close relative.

6. One. A slow, fair-haired person with a large mouth.

7. As many times as you have already had lovers.

8. Attractive and in the prime of life.

9. That you are amusing.

10. Trust no one blindly in this world.

11. Yes, and hopes that it is returned.

12. He or she thinks that you are dying of love for them.

13. You have already been in love a dozen times. You may be another dozen.

14. In three to four years.

15. Storms and calms by the score.

16. You will never want, so long as you remain industrious.

17. No, but by keeping it secret you will bring upon yourself many disagreeable consequences.

18. You would look better if you smiled more often.

19. Witty and amusing.

20. If not, it will be through no fault of your own.

21. Yes, but as quietly as possible.

22. At the next party you attend.

23. Not for a long time.

24. The one with the soft eyes.
25. Very soon, from the one you love.
26. Yes, and it will have a decisive effect on your life.
27. If you act prudently in a critical moment which is at hand, it will.
28. Yes, and you'll wish it hadn't been.
29. Writing a love letter.
30. A politician.
31. If it happens without your interference, it will cause much happiness to you.
32. It will come one day, but not yet.

 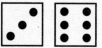

Nine

1. Only as one thinks of a small, insignificant creature.
2. Yes, a sailor. But this sailor is heir to a fortune.
3. Do what is asked of you.
4. No! It would turn out very badly.
5. Better not to, though it would do no real harm.
6. Three; one rich and two poor.
7. Once, to someone who will remain completely under your thumb.
8. A wearying person, with little energy.
9. That you are fairly attractive, and that if he or she could love anyone, it would be you.
10. Although a flirt, towards you the intentions are honorable.

11. You are their first and only love.

12. He or she imagines it's possible, at times, because they desperately want it to be so.

13. For at least two more years.

14. Within five years.

15. When you are traveling, not any other time.

16. If you always watch the pennies.

17. Nothing is so carefully hidden that it doesn't eventually come to light.

18. You are considered near perfect in looks.

19. Somewhat thoughtless but good at heart.

20. Yes, and you will live happily ever after.

21. There is certainly danger in it, but if you are careful, there is no real reason why you should not.

22. This very day.

23. Not before you have written one.

24. The first to confess love for you.

25. Yes, from someone you can't stand.

26. You will certainly have the opportunity.

27. Not for a very long time.

28. Yes, but it will break someone's heart.

29. Writing a letter, but not to you.

30. A wealthy person.

31. Yes.

32. This very day.

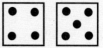

Nine

1. You are in their thoughts by day and dreams by night.
2. Not for a very long time.
3. Be gentle and patient and do not contradict.
4. It's now immaterial—tears will flow whether you do or not.
5. If you do, you will later regret it.
6. One tall, slender, handsome person with dark eyes.
7. Once, to a real tyrant.
8. Congenial but apt to overeat.
9. That you are still quite childish in many ways.
10. You would deeply hurt him or her if you didn't.
11. You cannot imagine just how much.
12. Yes…you along with all the rest!
13. You will fall in love very soon, after some unhappiness.
14. Within six years.
15. Yes, many.
16. Not very.
17. Not for a while.
18. Your face is considered your greatest asset.
19. Possibly.
20. If it were not for a very bitter enemy of his or hers.
21. If you do, there will be many tears…both of sorrow and of joy.
22. Only if you make the first move.
23. No, the people you want to hear from are all preoccupied.

24. The one who will stumble when next with you.
25. Yes, but an insignificant one.
26. You will certainly not want for invitations.
27. Not in any matter of importance.
28. Yes, but it will make many enemies.
29. Buying new clothes.
30. A military person.
31. No.
32. Tomorrow possibly, if not, then by next week.

Ten

1. Yes, and affectionately.
2. Why do you ask? They are already on their knees before you!
3. Try not to make a joke out of everything. Some things need to be treated seriously.
4. Reflect on what that might lead to.
5. Do so as though it's unimportant, and you'll come to no harm.
6. At least three.
7. One short, one tall, and one medium height.
8. Short and with a large nose.
9. You were always thought to be an angel, but now it appears there's a bit of the devil in you.
10. Try for as long as you honestly feel you can.
11. Without you all would be darkness.
12. Yes, but it is thought that you also love others.

13. Very soon you will fall in love with someone you thought you couldn't stand.

14. Not for seven years.

15. Many, and when you least expect to.

16. For a short time, but your foolishness will impoverish you.

17. No.

18. At times, with certain expressions, you are captivating.

19. No one would dispute it.

20. Yes, but you won't be as happy as you thought possible.

21. It really doesn't matter one way or the other.

22. There has been a misunderstanding that will take time to heal.

23. Very soon. A very nice letter.

24. The stoutest.

25. Not for some time.

26. A very long one.

27. When you decide it should be.

28. Yes, but it will cause envy—and that will bring you sorrow.

29. Making plans that do not include you.

30. Someone connected with the sea.

31. A blessing to you, and a delight to your friends.

32. Not the wished for, but very different news.

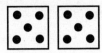

Ten

1. Not yet.
2. Someone desperately wants to and hopes to.
3. Whatever you do, you won't be able to do enough.
4. Meditate on whether it would be right.
5. If it will give you pleasure, yes.
6. Three, one whose name starts with a "W."
7. Once, to someone you already know, whose name starts with a "J."
8. A very funny person, full of tricks and jokes.
9. "If I only knew what to do to gain favor."
10. Test carefully first before trusting fully.
11. In secret, but may never say so out loud.
12. Yes, but is afraid you may not.
13. It's not free at the moment, but will be free again very soon.
14. This year.
15. One big one very soon.
16. Yes, but you must handle money carefully or you will lose it.
17. Very soon.
18. You look better in the evening than you do earlier in the day.
19. You can sometimes be very silly, but people generally overlook that, knowing you will grow out of it.
20. No, for they will never marry.
21. Do it and enjoy it!

22. It's possible that you may never meet again.
23. In a few days.
24. The one who laughs most easily.
25. Possibly tomorrow, though there may be a delay.
26. Yes, across the ocean.
27. Somewhat, and agreeably.
28. That will depend on your behavior.
29. Thinking of you and longing to be with you.
30. A medical person.
31. It will, at least, cause you many happy hours.
32. Unless you work towards it, no, never.

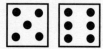

Eleven

1. Yes, but with some bitterness.
2. Someone you will meet within the next three days.
3. Whatever you like, for there's really no pleasing them.
4. At least wait for a letter to arrive before answering.
5. If you do, the person who asked will then laugh at you.
6. Two; one distantly related.
7. Once, to the person you now consider the least likely.
8. A good-for-nothing who will bring you nothing but trouble.
9. That you are an enigma.
10. Not too much. Be cautious.
11. Truly and faithfully.
12. He or she is too jealous to be certain.

13. No, it will shortly be stolen.

14. Before next winter.

15. Not soon, but in due course.

16. You could become so if you put your mind to it

17. You have nothing to fear.

18. Only by your lover.

19. Your heart is pure and your mind is clear.

20. Of course!

21. Consider first whether or not anyone would get harmed.

22. Yes, very unexpectedly.

23. Tomorrow.

24. The one with the snub nose.

25. Yes, very soon.

26. A delightful journey westward.

27. Not as soon as you expect nor in the way you expect.

28. If you really wish it, yes.

29. Reading one of your letters.

30. A tradesperson.

31. It is extremely doubtful.

32. Very soon, but all your expectations will not be gratified.

Twelve

1. Yes, though he or she is afraid of getting carried away with such thoughts.

2. An older person.

3. Let your love see that you return their love.

4. Yes, but in a cheerful, laughing way.

5. It will be a step with important consequences.

6. Many, but none of them serious.

7. However many times, it would be better if it were none.

8. Handsome and brilliant. You will be made for each other.

9. That you are overly sentimental.

10. Who else if not?

11. As much as you love them.

12. He or she thinks it's impossible, yet hopes it's so.

13. Not for more than a year.

14. When cats lay eggs!

15. You are too cautious.

16. You will always have as much as you have at present.

17. There is someone amongst your friends who will betray you.

18. As a beautiful flower.

19. You are thought to be thoughtless.

20. Don't let go. In the end there will be surrender.

21. If you can without being embarrassed.

22. Before the spring.

23. In a few weeks, a long one.

24. The one you met by chance.

25. Someone is considering giving you one, but is undecided.

26. Yes, to Europe.

27. Very soon and drastically.

28. Not entirely.
29. Longing to be with you.
30. An artist.
31. Decidedly. You will be very happy because of it.
32. The tidings are close at hand and will be more agreeable than you could hope.

Dominoes

Somewhat akin to dice are dominoes. Many Gypsy *vardos* hold a set of dominoes. It's a good game for passing the time, and also a means of earning money by *dukkerin'* with them. There are at least two ways of working with them.

Past/Present/Future

One thing that makes dominoes unique for fortune telling is that, in this method at least, two or three people can have their fortune told at the same time.

The dominoes are spread out over the table, face down, and generally mixed. Up to three people may then draw off three dominoes each. They draw them with their left hand and place them, still face down, in a line, horizontally, in front of them.

The domino on the Querent's left represents the past, that in the middle—the present, that on the right—the future.

Turning them over, they are interpreted as follows:

Sixes: Connected, in a general way, with good luck.

Fives: Refers to jobs and careers.

Fours: Deals with money matters.

Threes: Deals with love and love affairs.

Twos: Refers to close friends and family.

Ones: Deals with journeys and travel.

Blanks: Refers directly to the Querent.

From these general meanings, it is easy to give a quick reading of the upturned dominoes. For example, suppose the first domino is a Two/Three, the second is a One/Five and the third a Four/Blank. You would say that in the past (first domino) the Querent had a lot of very close family and friends with much love all around. At present (second one) the Querent is having to do a lot of traveling in connection with his or her job. And in the future (third), the Querent is going to have to give serious consideration to finances as they affect him or her personally.

In addition to these simple meanings, however, there are some special "double" combinations that must be considered:

Double-Six: The marriage of the Querent. If already married, then good fortune coming as the result of a wedding.

Double-Five: A promotion at work, to a higher and better paid position.

Double-Four: Unexpected money coming in a dramatic way.

Double-Three: The Querent will be falling in love unexpectedly.

Double-Two: Development of new friends who will become very close and dear.

Double-One: A wonderful vacation or journey that will be thoroughly enjoyable.

Double-Blank: This is one domino that is considered very unlucky. The Querent should exercise extreme caution in all things.

The Seven Veils

This is a reading done for a single Querent, using all the dominoes. Again they are laid out, face down, and "shuffled" by the Querent. One domino is drawn, turned up, and interpreted, then returned to the set, face down again. They are once more shuffled, and a second domino is chosen. This is interpreted and returned, face down. For a third time they are mixed, and one is picked and read. This is done up to a total of seven times. But it doesn't have to be seven; it could be only six, four, one, or any number less than seven that is chosen and read. It may not be *more* than seven, however. If the same domino is drawn more than once, it is an indication that the forces at work are very strong and the event will happen very soon.

In this form of reading, here are individual meanings given to each domino:

Double-Blank: A dull life; can also be an indication of loss and unhappiness.

One-Blank: Encounter with a stranger who will cause some unhappiness.

Two-Blank: The start of a new partnership, but it will lead nowhere, or to unhappiness.

Three-Blank: Problems brought about by jealousy and/or wrong decisions.

Four-Blank: You will receive a letter bearing bad news.

Five-Blank: You will attend a funeral, though not of a relative.

Six-Blank: Guard yourself against scandal. Possibility of scandal spread by someone you thought to be a friend.

How some Gypsies carry their dominoes.

Double-One: Now is the time to make a bold decision; things are perfectly in balance.

Two-One: You will lose money or property in the near future.

Three-One: An unexpected discovery; a pleasant surprise.

Four-One: Time to pay your debts if you are to stay out of trouble.

Five-One: The chance for a passionate, romantic love affair.

Six-One: Decision time…this could be the start or end of all you have dreamed of.

Double-Two: Both your home life and your business life are on solid ground. Beware of upsetting either boat.

Three-Two: Avoid taking any chances, especially gambling. You would be the loser.

Four-Two: Your investments, both in business and in life/love, will double.

Five-Two: Increase…profits in business or a child born.

Six-Two: You will receive a gift that will be extremely useful to you.

Double-Three: The marriage of an ex-love will aggravate you.

Four-Three: You will meet an ex-love you had all but forgotten.

Five-Three: A promotion.

Six-Three: You will be invited to a party. If you go, you will thoroughly enjoy it.

Double-Four. Unexpected money coming in a dramatic way.

Five-Four: A gamble pays off, but don't push your luck.

Six-Four: You will be involved in a lawsuit. Be cautious.

Double-Five: Relocation, to your great advantage.

Six-Five: You are in a position to help others. It would be good to do so.

Double-Six: Success in all things.

• ❧ •

9

Moles

Gypsies are very superstitious when it comes to moles on the body. It is thought that they are very positive indications of character and of events to come.

The larger the mole, the greater the prosperity or adversity that will come. If the mole is round, it signifies good; if oblong, a moderate share of good fortune; if angular, a fair mix of good and bad. The deeper the color of the mole, the more pronounced the effect, be it good or bad.

Moles on different parts of the body have different meanings, as follows:

Forehead: If a mole is in the center of the forehead, it predicts an active, industrious disposition with success in business and a happy marriage. But if the mole is on the side of the forehead, it's not so favorable, particularly on the left side. On the right side, or temple, it shows an industrious disposition with an interest in love and lovemaking; a great success in life generally, with a much-loved marriage partner.

On the left side, much the same, but far harder work will be needed in all areas to achieve the same success.

Eyebrows: A mole on the right eyebrow signifies a sprightly, active disposition; courage and perseverance. There will be wealth and success in love, business, and war. You will marry an agreeable mate and live happily, with many children. On the left eyebrow, it shows an indolent, peevish temper; a leaning towards alcohol; cowardice; and little interest in love per se. You will experience many disappointments in life and have no children.

Eyes: A mole on the outside corner of either eye shows a sober, honest, and steady disposition, much inclined to the pleasures of love. It also foretells a violent death after a life of ups and downs.

Nose: Moles on any part of the nose show a hasty and passionate disposition; you are much given to amorous pursuits. You are faithful, open, and sincere in your friendships. You tend to be petulant and tempted by alcohol. You will be successful throughout life and will "marry well," if not necessarily happily.

Cheek: On either cheek, a mole shows an industrious, benevolent person. Little inclined to athletic sports, yet very courageous. You will become neither rich nor very poor, but will be better off than your parents were.

Ear: On either ear, a mole denotes riches. If on the lower tip of the ear, stay away from water; there is a chance of drowning.

Lips: A mole on either lip shows a delicate person who must watch their diet and curb their appetite. Their health will always need attention.

Chin: An amiable and quiet disposition. Very agreeable and friendly. Industrious and with a love of travel. Highly successful in business. A good partner in business or life.

Neck: In front of the neck is a good sign; on the back of the neck is misfortune. On either side, it foretells that you will become quarrelsome and devious as you grow older.

Shoulder: On the left shoulder, a person who is quarrelsome and inclined to dispute anything and everything. It indicates a life that varies little, almost to the point of monotony. There will be many children and moderate success in business. On the right shoulder, it shows a person who is prudent and discreet, one with much wisdom and great tact and diplomacy. Very industrious but not too amorous. Would make a very good partner in anything.

Armpit: You are very good looking and will become rich and benevolent.

Arm: On either arm it indicates a courteous disposition, together with fortitude, resolution, and fidelity. In men, it also indicates that he will fight many battles and be successful in them all. It also shows a leaning to generosity and prosperity.

Elbow: A mole on either elbow shows a restless and unsteady disposition with a great desire to travel. Discontent with marriage; no great interest in amassing personal possessions. Friendly and faithful in friendship.

Wrist: You are ingenious; an inventor; an "idea" person.

Hand: Moles on either hand, so long as they are not on the fingers, denote wealth, industry, and energy generally, in either sex.

Fingers: On any finger, it is an indication that you will be a thief and never be wealthy.

Back: If below the shoulder blades, you will have a hard life, with many disappointments. If above the shoulder blades, you will face many challenges but rise to defeat them.

Buttocks: Signifies shiftlessness and probable poverty. You will tend to be lazy.

Chest: A quarrelsome and unhappy temper. You are extremely amorous and can become uncontrollable.

Breasts: A mole on the right breast shows you are given to drink and can become overly amorous. You will have many sudden reversals in your fortunes. Beware of pretended friends. A mole on the left breast shows that you are industrious and of sober disposition. Slow to arouse, but you can be a good lover. You will have much success in life and many children.

Nipple: In a woman, it is a sign that she will have a child who will become famous. In a man, it denotes that he will be fond of women and spend too much time pursuing them.

Side: On either side, near the ribs, it shows a cowardly disposition. You are given to excess in all things. You will have a relatively easy life, though not a luxurious one.

Hip: A mole on either hip shows a contented disposition. You are industrious, amorous, and very faithful to family and friends. You will have moderate success in life. All you receive you will have earned.

Navel: On a woman, it denotes many children and a good marriage. On a man, it is a sign that he will be lucky in all he undertakes, will become rich, and will have a son who will be distinguished.

Stomach: If on the pit of the stomach it shows a person who is somewhat foppish, with little common sense. It also denotes riches. If lower on the stomach, it's a sign that you will promise more than you will perform, but will, nevertheless, be held in high esteem.

Genitals: A generous, honest, and open disposition. Well mannered and gallant. A lover of love (rather than of sex) though not to excess. You will have a very happy marriage and, although you may not become rich, you will never want for anything. A woman with a mole on the *mons* will become the mother of a great genius.

Groin: On the right groin, it denotes riches and honors but to be accompanied by disease. On the left groin, you will have the sickness without the wealth.

Thigh: On the right thigh, it shows a person with an agreeable temper, inclined to be amorous, and very courageous. On the left thigh, it shows a person who is good and benevolent, hard working, and with no great interest in the pleasures of love-making.

Knee: On the left knee, it shows a hasty and passionate disposition, extravagance, no great leaning towards hard work nor honesty. On the right, it indicates an amiable temper, honest disposition, great success in love, and many good friends.

Leg: Moles on either leg show a person who is thoughtless and given to extravagance. There will be many difficulties throughout life, usually brought about by your own actions. In general, you will have more fortune than misfortune, but you will tend to remember, and dwell upon, the bad more than the good.

Ankle: Effeminacy in men, with a certain amount of cowardice. However, in women, it is a sign of courage.

Foot: A mole on either foot shows a melancholy disposition. Very inactive. Little inclined to do anything, not even follow the desires of your heart. Moles on the feet frequently foretell sickness and unexpected misfortune, with much sorrow.

Heel: A spiteful and malevolent disposition, but a person full of energy.

Instep: You will be quarrelsome and have few friends. You will be a great walker.

Toes: You will marry someone rich but be very unhappy.

10

Fire
Reading

The *Rom* spend many long hours sitting around the *yag* at the *atchen' tan*—the campfire. It's hardly surprising, then, that they can use that fire for divining. Gazing through half-closed eyes, almost dreamily, into the glowing embers, they are frequently able to make contact with…what? Their inner sight? The universal unconscious? Race memories? To connect with others' thoughts in what is generally termed Extra Sensory Perception? Whatever the label you care to use, the Gypsies themselves don't attempt to explain it. As with so many things, they just accept it as part of their natural selves.

Any number of people can read their own fortunes in the same fire, for the formations of the embers appear differently to each person, and are also interpreted by that person in their own individual way. This is the sort of divination that, although someone else can do it for you, it's probably far better you do it for yourself.

If you *are* doing it for someone else (a client), then sit with that person on your left; the client's right hand held between your own two hands as you gaze into the fire. Spend a few moments attuning to that person before focusing your gaze into the fire itself.

It may be that, no matter how long you gaze into the fire, you can see nothing that seems to have any real meaning to you. This is not necessarily an unfavorable sign but simply means that the forces at work are presently changing rapidly and have not settled into any sort of a complete picture. Give up and try again the next night, when they may have stabilized. Don't fire-gaze for longer than ten minutes at any one time.

Interpretation

How to interpret what you see? You can do no better than to follow the advice I gave for reading tea leaves (see Chapter 4).

You represent the client, so those symbols closest to you (as with the handle of the teacup) will be the ones which most affect the client.

Time is judged by position: any symbol near the top of the fire is in the present; the lower down the fire it appears, the further into the future it will be.

Those symbols on the left of the fire are more likely to be negative symbols, while those on the right are more likely to be positive.

Also as in tea leaf reading, the way a symbol faces may well have a specific meaning, particularly as to positive or negative influence.

To reiterate: don't expect all the symbols to look exactly like the things they represent. You will have to use your imagination a great deal. You will find that there is usually just a suggestion of, say, a bird or a rabbit or whatever. These suggestions are enough to trigger your mind into seeing them. Use the symbols simply as a focal point and go with your psychic feelings. Review all the meanings I gave for tea leaf reading and apply those to the images in the fire.

One final tip: if the fire has died down a lot, and you find that the embers are getting very dull, simply throw a handful of salt onto the fire. It will cause it to flare up again long enough for you to complete your reading.

• ᴄꙄᴏ •

11

Crystals and Gemstones

In the popular mind, Gypsies wear a great deal of gold and silver: bracelets and necklaces, gold coins (especially as decoration on clothing), and many silver and gold rings on the fingers. This isn't an incorrect picture, certainly of Gypsies in the past, but the reason for it is not ostentation. These days the *Rom* are perhaps not quite so obvious, but still do keep their money to themselves. The reason is simply that they do not trust the *gaujo's* banks. That and the fact that in the days before twenty-four hour money machines, and chains of banks across the country, they never knew when they would be anywhere near a bank. It was therefore much more convenient (and, to their eyes, safer) to keep their money about their person. Not only do they keep their wealth in coin but also in jewels.

Vest of a Gypsy dukkerer.

There is a tremendous interest today in crystals, precious and semi-precious stones. Gypsies have always been aware of their occult significance. They wear them and carry them and use them, not as followers of a current fad but as keepers of the Romani Mysteries. Here I will simply detail how such stones are used by them for divination.

First, let's look at the popular beliefs in the properties of the major stones, together with their meanings when used for Romani divination. (See page 186 for divination instructions.)

Agate: Also known as "Scotch Pebble." This is a semi-precious stone with bands of color, usually brown, dark red or yellow, or sometimes blue or green. It's associated with people born in the astrological sign of Gemini. An old rhyme goes:

Who comes with the summer to this earth,
And owes to June her hour of birth,
With ring of agate on her hand
Can wealth, health and long life command.

Agate is supposed to be especially lucky for farmers, foresters, gardeners, and all connected with the land. It gives strength to the heart and will cure snake bites.

For Romani divination, agate represents a pleasant surprise.

Amethyst: A variety of quartz, with purple, violet, or mauve coloring. It is associated with Aquarians. The old rhyme is:

The February born shall find
Sincerity and peace of mind,
Freedom from passion and from care,
If they the amethyst will wear.

The stone is most popularly associated with drunkenness. If an amethyst is placed in a glass of water and allowed to steep there, the water can later be drunk and will cure the drunkenness. The stone is also lucky for lovers and brings faithfulness in love to those who wear it, also freedom from jealousy and anger. Additionally it is good for counteracting magickal charms.

The Romani divination meaning is that you will lose something of value.

Bloodstone: A semi-precious stone which is dark green with red spots that look like small bloodstains. It was thought that it had the power to stop bleeding. Associated with those born under the sign of Pisces, the rhyme goes:

Who on this world of ours their eyes
In March first open, shall be wise,
In days of peril strong and brave,
And wear a bloodstone to their grave.

Many soldiers used to carry such a stone into battle with them. It was said to ward off illness and give courage to its wearer.

The Romani meaning for divination is that there will be an unpleasant surprise coming.

Diamond: A pure form of carbon, usually crystal clear and very sparkling. It is said to be luckiest when worn on the left side. Associated with Aries, the rhyme is:

She who from April dates her years,
Diamonds shall wear, lest bitter tears
For vain repentance flow. This stone
Emblem of innocence is known.

It symbolizes strength, virtue, and bravery and also insight. Worn around the neck, it ensures safe childbirth. Gypsies believe that it will lose its sparkle if touched by the hand of a traitor.

The divinatory meaning is of a business advancement.

Emerald: A precious stone of the beryl type, but distinguished from beryl by its beautiful green color. Associated with Taurus, the rhyme is:

Who first beholds the light of day
In spring's sweet, flowery month of May,
And wears an emerald all her life.
Shall be a loved and loving wife.

The emerald was supposed to be good for eyesight and also to strengthen memory. Romani lore says that if given by one lover to another, it will pale and grow dull if love should fade between them.

Its meaning in divination is a secret admirer.

Garnet: A semi-precious stone, usually red or reddish brown, sometimes yellow, black, or green. It brings a healthy and cheerful disposition and is associated with the sign of Capricorn.

By her who in this month was born
No gem save garnets shall be worn.
They will ensure her constancy,
True friendship and fidelity.

Garnets are also believed to ward off inflammatory diseases. Divination meaning is that you will receive a letter.

Opal: A precious stone of cloudy white that flashes with rainbow hues as it catches the light. For the Libra:

> *October's child is born for woe,*
> *And life's vicissitudes must know;*
> *But lay an opal on her breast,*
> *And hope will lull those woes to rest.*

For other than the Libran, it is considered an unlucky stone to wear in an engagement ring. The Gypsies say that for anyone else, the marriage will never take place. For those whose birthstone it is, however, it will give the power of second sight. As with the emerald, it will lose its brilliance if worn by an unfaithful lover.

Romani divination meaning is of death—not necessarily to the Querent—but certainly to someone close to them.

Ruby: Considered by many to be the most precious of all jewels. Except for the color, it is the same in composition as sapphire with similar brilliance. It is usually thought of as being a glowing red, but it may range between pink and almost violet. The jewel for Cancer.

> *The glowing ruby shall adorn*
> *Those who in warm July are born.*
> *Then will they be exempt and free*
> *From love's doubt and anxiety.*

The ruby is good for cases of poisoning (used as was the amethyst for drunkenness). It gets rid of depression and all evil thoughts. It brings good fortune and friendship.

In divination, ruby indicates the influence of a stranger.

Sapphire: A precious stone which is usually a clear corn-flower blue. The stone of Virgo.

A maiden born when autumn leaves
Are rustling in September's breeze,
A sapphire on her brow should bind;
'Twill cure diseases of the mind.

This gem is lucky for lovers and brings peaceful, optimistic happiness. It is good for inflammation of the eyes and generally attracts good fortune.

The meaning in Romani divination is that a wrong done in the past will catch up with the Querent.

Sardonyx: A variety of onyx that has white and dark red or white and dark brown markings in bands or layers. It is associated with Leo.

Wear a sardonyx or for thee
No conjugal felicity.
The August-born without this stone,
'Tis said, must live unloved alone.

Protecting against the bite of snakes, sardonyx also brings happiness to married couples.

The divinatory meaning is that there will be a wedding in the future, though not necessarily of the Querent.

Topaz: A more or less transparent precious stone which is usually clear yellow but sometimes yellowish white, blue, or even pink. The stone of Scorpio.

Who first comes to this world below
In drear November's fog and snow,
Should prize the topaz' amber hue,
Emblem of friends and lovers true.

Gypsies consider it good for warding off chest complaints, rheumatic troubles, and asthma. It is also considered to bring fidelity in love and friendship.

The meaning in divination is that caution needs to be exercised.

Turquoise: A translucent or opaque precious stone of a blue or blue-green color. Its coloring and luster vary with the feelings of the wearer. Associated with Sagittarius, the old rhyme goes:

> *If cold December gave you birth,*
> *The month of snow and ice and mirth,*
> *Place on your hand a turquoise blue,*
> *Success will bless whate'er you do.*

The stone protects from danger and misfortune. When the wearer is near death, the stone will fade to a very pale shade.

In divination, it is the sign of an imminent journey.

Significator and Layouts

These twelve are the stones most generally used for divination—these or suitable substitutes (e.g., clear quartz for diamond; amber for topaz). A circle of roughly eighteen inches in diameter is drawn on the ground or table. A rough, ordinary stone is taken from the ground in the vicinity of where the divination is being done. This is placed with the other stones and will serve as the Significator. The Querent will then take all thirteen stones in his or her hands, shake them together, and throw them into the circle. If the Significator stone rolls outside the circle, the Querent must throw them again. If it rolls out a second time, no fortune can be told for twenty-four hours.

The stones are read according to their relationship to one another and to the Significator. Whether or not the stones are interpreted as Sun signs or purely according to their divinatory meanings seems up to the feelings of the dukkerer. For example, supposing that the Significator falls next to the ruby and close to the topaz. The diviner might say that the Querent should exercise caution (topaz) when a stranger tries to influence him or her (ruby), or that the Querent should be cautious should he or she come into contact with a person born under the sign of Cancer (of course, it may well be that the stranger is a Cancer!).

All the stones need to be studied according to how they fall, and their relationship to one another. Positioning within the circle has bearing on the time frame. The closer to the center of the circle, the closer to the present. The closer to the edge of the circle, the further into the future.

Some Gypsies do not use the Significator stone. They follow the instructions as described above except for the Significator and the time frame, which is read differently. They draw two lines across the circle, at approximately one-third intervals, and take the closest area as the present, the center section as the near future (within about six months) and the furthest section as the far distant future (see illustration below). Relative position to the center line indicates relative influence on the Querent.

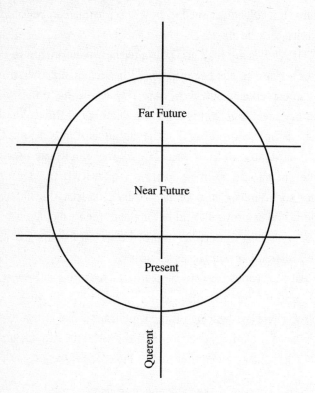

**Gemstone layout for divination without
the Significator stone.**

• ∾ •

12

Sticks
and Stones

Kosh, or *kosht*, is Romanes for "stick," and *bar* is the word for "stone." *Dukkerin' kosht* is therefore the true name for divining with sticks, and *dukkerin' bars* for divining with stones.

Sticks (*Koshes*)

I have seen many Gypsies in the southwest of England *dukkerin' kosht*; it seems to be little known in the north, however. [I gave a version of this based on the *Rom* variety in my books *Buckland's Complete*

Book of Witchcraft (Llewellyn, 1986) and *The Tree: Complete Book of Saxon Witchcraft* (Weiser, 1974). In those I called it "Saxon Wands."]

Seven sticks are needed for this. They are usually cut from the hedgerow (or a convenient bush) and are nothing special other than being more or less straight. Four of the sticks should be longer than the other three. I'd suggest the three be at about nine inches in length and the four at about twelve inches. One of the twelve-inch ones should be much thicker than the others. This one is referred to as the *kralisi* ("Queen").

To use them, you lay the *kralisi* on the ground horizontally in front of you. Take the other six sticks and hold them out over the *kralisi*. Close your eyes and concentrate on the question you need answered. Rub your hands together to mix up the sticks. Keeping your eyes closed, grip all the sticks in your right hand and then take hold of the tip of one of them with your left hand. Open your right hand and let the sticks fall, except for the one your left hand is holding.

You will see—on opening your eyes—that the five sticks have fallen on or over the *kralisi*. Here is how you interpret the way they have fallen:

1. If there are more of the *longer* sticks than the shorter ones on the ground, then the answer is in the affirmative.

2. If there are more of the *shorter* ones than the longer ones (excluding the *kralisi*), then the answer is in the negative.

3. If any sticks actually *touch* the *kralisi*, it indicates that the answer will be a very positive one, or will take place in a very positive way, with strong forces at work.

4. If any sticks are *off the ground*, resting on others, then regardless of 1 or 2, no definite answer can be given at this time, for things are still "up in the air."

5. If all the sticks point *toward* the *kralisi*, then the Querent will have a very definite part to play in the determination of the question.

6. If *none* of the sticks point *toward* the *kralisi*, then the matter will be determined with no involvement on the part of the Querent.

This is a simple, yet effective, method of getting an answer to a question. By choosing your question(s) carefully, you can often narrow a problem down till you've completely solved it. As with all Romani divination, *dukkerin'* kosht is of an extremely practical nature, using the simplest of tools yet providing positive answers.

Stones (*Bars*)

Dukkerin' bars are used a great deal for getting "Yes/No" answers to questions. It is similar, in this respect, to the use of the pendulum (see Chapter 13 on needle divination) but is much easier.

A Gypsy will pick up two small round stones, somewhere between the size of an acorn and a walnut. (They don't have to be found at the same time. In fact it's not uncommon to search for a very long time before finding the two that seem "just right" for the individual.) One should be white or light in color, and the other black or dark, and they should both be of approximately the same shape and size. These are carefully washed, and from then on usually carried in a little bag hung from the belt or on a thong around the neck.

To use the stones, they are simply cupped in the hands and shaken like dice, while the question to be answered is concentrated on. They are then thrown down. If they land with the white stone closer to the thrower than the dark stone, then the answer is in the positive. If they land with the dark stone closer, then the answer is in the negative. If they land side by side, equidistant, then the question must be asked again or rephrased. *Dukkerin' bars* are as simple as that.

13

Knives and Needles

There are two very simple forms of divining that are used a lot by Gypsy children (*chavvies*), as well as by their elders. At first glance they may seem little more than parlor games, yet they can provide answers to questions as well as many far more complicated methods. The first of these is by spinning a knife.

Knives

Amongst their kitchen utensils, many Gypsy *vardos* include a round wooden bread board, about twelve inches in diameter. These are most commonly used for the knife divination. A round salver, or tray, will do just as well. If nothing else, cut out a circle from a sheet of cardboard.

A regular kitchen knife is used and is placed in the center of the board. Around the edges of the board are placed pieces of paper (about two inches long by an inch or so wide) on which have been written suitable "answers." Some of the most commonly used ones are:

- Yes.
- No.
- You must have patience.
- Beware of false friends.
- Good news is coming.
- A letter is expected.
- Success in business.
- An unexpected visitor.
- Love is here.
- Tears will turn to joy.
- News from abroad.
- A new admirer.
- An unexpected meeting.
- A journey.
- An important letter.

The question is concentrated upon, then the Querent spins the knife by its center. It is twirled three times in all, giving three answers. Of these, one (though not necessarily the first received) will be an answer to the original question, while the other two will be additional answers which may or may not be related to it.

Front of a bow-top vardo.

Should the knife stop equidistant between two of the answers, then that spin can be discounted and the knife spun again.

Needles

Divining with common sewing needles is very simple indeed. Twenty-one new needles are placed in a saucer or plate. Water is then slowly poured on them. However gently the water is poured, it will be found that the needles move. The Gypsies say that the number of needles that cross each other indicates the number of enemies, or forces, working against you that you will encounter that month (Moon's period).

A needle may also be used as a pendulum. The needle is threaded with red silk thread (approximately nine inches long). The end of the thread is then held, with the needle hanging down, and questions are asked.

The client is asked for a coin (a silver coin was tradition-al…a quarter will do!). This is placed on the table. You sit with the end of the thread in your hand, elbow resting on the table, and the needle suspended just above the coin. The client may ask as many questions as he or she wishes, though they should be questions that can be answered "Yes" or "No" only. You should try to keep your hand quite still, yet you will find that as you concentrate on the question, the needle will start to swing.

A swing backwards and forwards, towards you and away from you, indicates "Yes." A swing across you indicates

"No." If the needle simply swings around in a circle, it means that the question is vague; it needs to be rephrased. If it hangs without swinging, then the question cannot be answered at this time.

For more sophisticated methods of using a pendulum, please see my book *Practical Color Magick* (Llewellyn, 1983).

• ∾ •

14

Omens and Portents

Bok and Kushti Bok

ok is bad luck, and *kushti bok* is good luck. I will give some of the major omens regarded by the Romani in England. It would take a huge book to contain all the many little signs and circumstances. I am certainly not going to deal here with such things as spilling salt, breaking mirrors, and walking under ladders. That is not to say that there is not "something to them"; it is just that they have been covered adequately in just about every book written that deals with superstitions.

Don't be too quick to laugh at some of the following beliefs. They are usually held after many generations' observance and are extremely valid; if not true one hundred percent of the time, then certainly a very high percentage.

It is considered an ill omen to see a spider early in the morning. The earlier in the morning, and the larger the spider, the greater the evil that threatens you. But it is only if the spider is indoors—and especially if in your bedroom—that it is so significant. Outdoors, it bodes no harm. Gypsies also say that this refers basically to the house spider. The wood spider is not to be dreaded. In fact, do not on any account kill a wood spider, or you will draw to you the hatred of the whole race of spiders and, sooner or later, would suffer by it.

When found in the evening, a spider signifies good luck. A *Rom* saying goes: "*Sarla, tugno. Rarti, doodani*"—literally, "Morning, sadness. Evening, shining" (or "hope"). The smaller the spider, the greater the good fortune. Tiny spiders have much less bad luck in them than the larger ones. Daddy longlegs are always messengers of *good* luck.

From time immemorial, the horseshoe has been considered a sign of luck. It is a blending of two elements—the shape of the shoe (that of a crescent moon) and the metal of the shoe (iron). As Dr. G. Storms points out in *Anglo-Saxon Magic* (Gordon Press, 1974), for millennia, iron has been considered magickal, partly from the mysterious way in which it was originally found in meteoric stones. Gypsies have a special regard for horses. In fact, it is not the dog but the horse that is considered the Gypsy's best friend. With all these elements, then, it is hardly surprising that the *Rom* consider the horseshoe a symbol for luck. Many a *vardo* will have a horseshoe hung over the entrance...hung with the points up, to hold in the luck. Incidentally, Horatio Nelson, the great eighteenth century English admiral, had such faith in the horseshoe that he always had one nailed to the main mast of his ship *Victory*.

If a Gypsy finds a horseshoe lying in the road with the points toward him, he will spit on it and throw it over his left shoulder. This is to counteract any bad luck that was held in the shoe and has now transferred from it to him.

If a horse rolls on the ground, rolling over and back again, this is a sign of good fortune coming, usually connected with money. To meet a red-headed person riding a white horse is extremely good luck.

In the north of England—good horse country—the *Rom* say that if a horse runs around neighing loudly, someone nearby is dying.

If your right ear tingles, or itches, someone is speaking well of you. If your left ear tingles, they are speaking ill of you. To find out who it is, call out loud the names of all those you think it could be. The tingling will stop when you call out the correct name.

If your nose itches early in the morning, you will receive good news later in the day. Gypsies in the west of England say that the itching nose means you will have company come to visit that day. A nosebleed is an omen of bad luck.

To accidentally put your left shoe on your right foot is a sure sign of an accident to come. Reginald Scott, in his *Discovery of Witchcraft* (London, 1584) says: "He that receiveth a mischance will consider whether he put not on his shirt

wrong side outwards, or his left shoe on his right foot."
Gypsies are not concerned about putting on their shirts
inside out, but they do take note of the wrong shoe.

To have a picture drop out of its frame, or to have a stone
fall out of its setting, is a very bad omen. If the picture is
that of a relative, it could mean the coming death of that relative. To remove a ring from your finger when you have had
it there a number of years is a portent of coming illness.

It is extremely unlucky to kill a ladybug, a swallow,
robin, or wren. To destroy the nest of one of the birds is
equally unlucky. Within the course of a year, the person
will break a bone.

If a flock of ducks flies across the road from left to right,
it is a fortunate sign; if they fly from right to left, unfortu-
nate. However, if a rabbit runs across your path from left to
right, that is unlucky. But you can put matters to rights,
apparently, by tearing some article of clothing!

To find a dead crow lying in a road or field is a sign of
good luck. But it is extremely unlucky to come across the
body of a dead owl.

I have many times seen my grandfather "tickling" trout.
He would lie on the riverbank, where the bank overhangs
slightly, and let his hand trail down in the water. Apparently
trout are fond of lazily floating in the shade provided by the
overhanging bank. With his fingers curled up, my grandfather would gently tickle the bellies of the fish, lulling them
into some sort of complacency. Then he would slip his fingers around the belly and, in one quick movement, jerk
them up out of the water and over onto the bank. I have
seen him catch a large number of trout this way. But then, in

true Gypsy style, he will always leave one of the fish hanging in a tree—to ensure that there will be good fishing there the next time.

It is very unlucky to hear the screech owl at night. This is considered by the Gypsies to be a most unlucky bird. An old pastoral poem by Francis Grose (1731-1791) goes:

> *Within my cot, where quiet gave me rest,*
> *Let the dread screech owl build her hated nest.*
> *And from my window o'er the country send*
> *Her midnight screams to bode my latter end.*

Weather Omens and Portents

There seem to be more weather omens than there could possibly be changes in the weather! First, let's look at omens in the sky itself.

If there is a change from continuing wet and stormy to clear and dry, and that change takes place at the time of either the New or the Full Moon (or close to), then it's likely to remain fine till the next quarter. Similarly, if there is no change in the weather at the quarters, then the existing weather will last for a week or two at least.

If there is a general mist at sunrise, or a "sheep sky" as the Gypsies call it, or white clouds drifting to the northwest, then it will be fine for several days.

If there are many clouds seen in the west at sunrise, and they soon disappear, then there will be fine weather but of short duration.

If there are red clouds in the west at sunset, it will be fine; if they have a tint of purple, it will be very fine.

If a layer of fine clouds comes up from the northwest underneath other higher clouds driving more south, then there will be fine weather for a short spell.

If there is lightning without thunder after a clear day, there will be a continuation of fair weather.

If there is a rainbow during wet weather, then the rain is passing from us.

If the clouds at sunrise are red, then there will be rain within twenty-four hours.

If the sun sets in dark heavy clouds, there will be rain the next day.

If there is a change of wind from west to south, or east to south, then it is going to be wet.

If the lower clouds drive more from the south than those above, it will be wet.

If the stars above forty-five degrees—especially the North Star—flicker strongly and appear closer than usual, there will be rain.

Let us look at animals and insects and their actions as portents for the weather—something my grandfather was excellent with.

If spiders, in spinning their webs, make the terminating filaments long (the anchoring lines), the weather will be fine for a number of days (the longer the filaments, the longer will the weather remain fine).

Spiders generally alter their webs every twenty-four hours. If they do so between six and seven o'clock in the evening, it will be a fine night. If they alter their webs in the morning, a fine day. If they work in the rain, you can expect it to clear up and be a nice day. The more active a spider is, the finer the weather will be.

If owls screech during foul weather, it will change to fair.

If gnats fly thickly in the setting Sun, expect warm weather. If they are seen a great deal in the spring, expect a warm fall.

A Gypsy saying from the southwest of England goes:

If a cock crow when he goes to bed,
He will arise with a very wet head.

If sheep and goats spring about and fight more than usual, expect rain. Similarly, if cattle leave off their feeding and chase one another, it is going to rain.

If horses stretch out their necks and sniff the air, and gather together in a corner of the field with their heads turned away from the wind, expect rain. Similarly, if they suddenly stop feeding and begin scratching themselves on trees and fences, there will be heavy rain.

If pigs grow restless and grunt loudly, and if they jerk up their heads, there will be a great deal of wind. If a pig picks up a piece of wood in its mouth, it's a sure sign of bad weather. In fact, Gypsies have a saying: "Pigs can see the wind."

Other indicators of coming rain are frogs and toads croaking more than usual; bees remaining in their hives or only flying a short distance away; worms coming out of the ground in numbers; swallows flying lower than usual; crows making a great deal of noise and flying around in circles; dogs eating grass; cats sneezing and/or washing their face and behind their ears; and fish biting more readily and splashing up at the surface of the water.

With flowers, if the marigold stays shut after seven in the evening, it is going to rain. If the convolvulus and chickweed close up, there'll be rain. If the leaves of the trees move without any perceptible breeze, it is going to rain. If oak trees bud earlier than ash trees in the spring, then you can expect a wet summer. If dew lies thickly on the grass after a fair day, it's a sure sign of another fair day coming.

As I have said, there are probably ten or a hundred times as many weather signs as I have given. Different parts of the country seem to favor different signs. The best thing is to study weather changes and keep a log of possible signs, verifying them over long periods. You'll find that soon a definite pattern will emerge.

• ∽ •

15

Cold
Reading

What happens when a client comes for a reading and you just aren't "in the mood?" Many *Rom* have to do readings in order to earn a living. If they are advertising their services and someone comes and pays money, they have to produce. But suppose they can't? Well, then they resort to what is often referred to as a "cold reading"—a reading that is not based on any psychic attunement, but is the result of astute observation and deduction; picking up clues from the appearance and reaction of the client. There may be a great deal of psychology involved; but then there generally is in any reading.

For doing a cold reading, some sort of "prop" is a good idea. It serves as a focal point for the client and looks as though the Reader really is going from something. The safest, and also the most impressive, is probably a large crystal ball. Too many clients have a knowledge of tarot cards these days to be able to use them simply as a prop. You might get away with regular playing cards, but as I say, a crystal is probably the safest and most impressive.

Here are just a few examples of some of the clues that may be picked up from the person who has come for a reading. When a client loudly boasts about something, he or she is probably frustrated in some desire(s) and feeling somewhat inferior. A dull, monotonous voice, with slow delivery, shows the client to be feeling defeated, rejected. If he or she speaks with rising inflection, then the client has some doubt about what you have said; the client is finding it hard to believe. Short, sharp sentences usually indicate excitement.

To give some generalizations—and that is all they can be—men are generally interested in prestige, be it money, position, or power. Women are frequently jealous and afraid their husband is being unfaithful. Young people are mostly interested in the opposite sex. Again, these are broad generalizations and also pretty sexist for today! However, these *are* very pertinent when it comes to the *type of people who frequent Gypsy Dukkerers*. Here are some of the reasons people do go to fortune tellers:

- Amusement.
- Frustration.

- Curiosity.
- Wish-fulfillment.
- Anxiety.
- Need for a confidant.

With this last one, many women use a fortune teller as many men use a bartender—a friendly stranger to whom they can pour out their problems. A great many of life's problems *can* be solved simply by verbalizing them, and certainly by getting unbiased input from another point of view. These are the sort of clients that the *Dukkerer* loves. No psychic work is actually called for, only good common sense! Just put yourself in the place of the client and decide what *you* would do under the circumstances.

As to anxiety…the vast majority of women who have their fortunes told are concerned that someone is "working against them." They believe that someone has placed a curse on them. There are many unscrupulous "Readers" who prey upon these people, encouraging them in this belief and promising to remove the curse—for a fee! Invariably, the curse is not removed "because it was stronger than thought," and there is call for a higher fee! This type of "fortune teller" does *dukkerin'* a great disservice. Please don't ever resort to what may seem like easy money and play off these susceptible people.

Continuing with the generalizations: the principal problems troubling the female center around love and security. The "love" here is not just love of the opposite sex, but also love of home, family, and friends. Security involves money and love security. Health, too, falls into the love category…the health of the woman herself and of her family and loved ones.

Much of this can be obvious to the Romani just by studying the client. For example, when a woman sits twisting her wedding band round and round on her finger, it is a good sign that she has a marriage problem. But frequently, the client will burst out with what is worrying her, telling all and just asking for advice (or "What do you see for me?").

Let's look at types for a moment.

An *attractive young girl* is frequently juggling and judging boyfriends, though it could be that she is unsure of herself and her own attractiveness. Which of these it is usually becomes quickly apparent.

The *plain, homely girl* is often afraid of the opposite sex and, indeed, afraid of sex itself. She may be dominated by her mother or trapped into a stay-at-home life.

An *older unmarried woman* (again remembering that we are talking about the type of people who habitually go to fortune tellers) is frequently frustrated and becoming desperate in her search for "Mr. Right." She is frequently lonely and, many times, bitter. A good clue to this type of woman is her use of sarcasm with regard to anything positive that you might suggest. Sometimes she is suspicious about her "friends"—are they really friends or are they talking behind her back?

The *wife and/or mother* frequently has many worries about whether or not her husband is faithful, about her children ("Are they into the drug scene?"), and about money and paying the bills.

The *young man* is most often troubled about the possible unfaithfulness of his girlfriend. As with the young girl, if the young man is a homely type, it's more likely that he is troubled by a lack of girlfriends.

The *businessman* usually has one of two problems (and seldom both together). Either he has a problem in business involving a deal, promotion, or decision; or he is trying to choose between his wife and his girlfriend.

Elderly people are most often concerned about family members, finances, or what will become of them.

(I cannot stress too strongly—knowing the justifiable sensitivity of many people today—that these are generalities and that they do *not*—by any means—apply to all who fall under these categories. However, what I have listed is true for the vast majority of such people who go looking for advice from a fortune teller.)

The client has a good idea of what he or she wants to hear before ever stepping into the *Dukkerer's ofisa* (office). Always give positive advice, never negative. We do create our own realities, so to put a positive future into the client's mind is to give him or her the ammunition to bring about what is really desired.

Flatter where possible, without being too obvious.

Here is a list of things you should consider when giving a cold reading:

- The physical health of the client.
- Their state (e.g., calm; nervous; chain smoking).
- Personality.
- Age.
- Marital state.
- Affluence.

Don't be afraid to ask questions of the client. "Do you have many friends?" is a natural question that may well lead to a whole opening up on the part of the client. "Do you suspect someone of working against you?" is another good one.

It can be useful to know the client's age, yet the client may be reluctant to divulge it. Here is a handy little device that will determine it for you. It works for anyone aged sixty or under. You make up a set of six cards as shown on pages 213 and 214.

Giving the cards to the client, ask him or her to pick out all the cards which contain their age, wherever that happens to be on the card. Take these cards the client has picked and quickly, mentally, add together all the numbers in the top right-hand corner of each card chosen. The total will be the client's age.

For example, suppose the client's age is twenty. He will pick out cards B and E—the only two cards with twenty on them. The top right-hand corner numbers are four and sixteen, respectively. Added together, these give the age: twenty.

Some *Dukkerers* have a small slip of paper they have the client fill out and sign at the start of the reading. The paper basically says that the client understands that the reading is purely for entertainment purposes. With some of the unfair laws against fortune telling still used in many states, it is perhaps a good and wise precaution to do this. The clients read it and sign it. Additionally, on this slip of paper, some *Dukkerers* have a line asking for birth month and day (not year, since some people seem sensitive to giving their age). The reason for this added line is that, if you know anything of astrology, by ascertaining the client's birth month and day (you don't need the year) you can then apply much of the

CARD A

3	5	7	9	11	1
13	15	17	19	21	23
25	27	29	31	33	35
37	39	41	43	45	47
49	51	53	55	57	59

CARD B

5	6	7	13	12	4
14	15	20	21	22	23
28	29	30	31	36	37
52	38	39	44	45	46
47	53	54	55	60	13

CARD C

9	10	11	12	13	8
14	15	24	25	26	27
28	29	30	31	40	41
42	43	44	45	46	47
56	57	58	59	60	13

**Three cards from a set of six used to determine
the age of a client.**
(See cards D-F on the following page.)

CARD D

3	6	7	10	11	2
14	15	18	19	22	23
26	27	30	31	34	35
38	39	42	43	46	47
50	51	54	55	58	59

CARD E

17	18	19	20	21	16
22	23	24	25	26	27
28	29	30	31	48	49
50	51	52	53	54	55
56	57	58	59	30	60

CARD F

33	34	35	36	37	32
38	39	40	41	42	43
44	45	46	47	48	49
50	51	52	53	54	55
56	57	58	59	60	41

**Three cards from a set of six used to determine
the age of a client.**
(See cards A-C on the previous page.)

"typical" Sun sign attributes to your client as part of the cold reading. A knowledge of astrology can certainly stand you in good stead where a cold reading is concerned. Incidentally, Gypsies don't generally practice either astrology or numerology (there are exceptions, of course), because they do not care to be bothered with math. They can count and do multiplication and division, but they are not generally "into numbers." Hence, I have not included either of these forms of divination in this book.

In *Gypsy Sorcery and Fortune Telling* (Fisher-Unwin, 1891), Charles Godfrey Leland gives some "rules" for cold readings. Not all of them are applicable today, yet many are. They are as follows:

> **1.** It is safe in most cases with middle-aged men to declare that they have had a lawsuit, or a great dispute as to property, which has given them a great deal of trouble. This must be impressively uttered. Emphasis and sinking the voice are of great assistance in fortune telling. If the subject betrays the least emotion, or admits it, promptly improve the occasion, express sympathy, and "work it up."
>
> **2.** Declare that a great fortune, or something greatly to the advantage of the subject, or something which will gratify him, will soon come in this way, but that he must be keen to watch his opportunity and be bold and energetic.
>
> **3.** He will have three great chances, or fortunes, in his life. If you *know* that he has inherited or made a fortune, or had a good appointment, you may say that he has already realized one of them. This seldom fails.
>
> **4.** A lady of great wealth and beauty, who is of singularly sympathetic disposition, is in love with him, or ready to be, and it will depend on him to secure his happiness. Or he will soon meet such a person when he shall least expect it.
>
> **5.** "You had at one time great trouble with your relations (friends). They treated you very unkindly." Or, "They were prepared to do so but your resolute conduct daunted them."

6. "You have been three times in great danger of death." Pronounce this very impressively. Everybody, though it be a schoolboy, believes or likes to believe that he has encountered perils. This is infallible, or at least it takes in most people. If the subject can be induced to relate his hairbreadth escapes, you may foretell future perils.

7. "You have had an enemy who has caused you great trouble. But he—or she—it is well not to specify which till you find out the sex—will ere long go too far and his or her effort to injure you will recoil on him or her." Or, briefly, "It is written that someone, by trying to wrong you, will incur terrible retribution." Or, "You have had enemies but they are all destined to come to grief." Or, "You had an enemy but you outlived him."

8. "You got yourself once into great trouble by doing a good act."

9. "Your passions have thrice got you into great trouble. Once your inconsiderate anger (or pursuit of pleasure) involved you in great suffering which, in the end, was to your advantage." Or else, "This will come to pass; therefore be on your guard."

10. "You will soon meet with a person who will have a great influence on your future life if you cultivate his friendship. You will ere long meet someone who will fall in love with you if encouraged."

11. "You will find something very valuable if you keep your eyes open and watch closely. You have twice passed over a treasure and missed it, but you will have a third opportunity."

12. "You have done a great deal of good, or made the fortune or prosperity of persons who have been very ungrateful."

13. "You have been involved in several love affairs, but your conduct in all was really perfectly blameless."

14. "You have great capacity for something, and before long an occasion will present itself for you to exert it to your advantage."

As Leland says, by stating these points carefully, sometimes combining some of them, the fortune teller can sound amazingly credible.

A few final points on cold readings:

Remember that human beings like to be flattered. Don't overdo it to become too obvious, but do flatter. Even if the client realizes that you are flattering, he or she will love you for it!

Speak fairly rapidly. This makes it difficult for the client to remember everything you say and will lead him or her to think things into the reading that in fact you did not discuss! A vivid imagination and eagerness on the part of the client will cover a lot of ignorance on your part.

Watch the client's reactions carefully. If you get off on the wrong track, it should soon become obvious from these reactions. It can help to periodically say something like, "There are many forces at work at the present time. If I make any important error as I read, please let me know at once, so that I do not follow a blind path."

Don't hesitate to ask a direct question. The answer can give you important information, which you can enlarge upon as though you had all of it originally.

Don't read for more than one person at a time and don't allow the client to have a friend or friends listening. You don't need an audience...or witnesses!

Don't do a cold reading unless you absolutely have to. Far better to do a true reading using those psychic abilities which we all do possess. Don't forget that the more you use them, the more they will develop.

For more on cold reading, pick up any good book dealing with body language. I would also strongly recommend the once popular book *Dr. Abravanel's Body Type Program* (Bantam Books, 1985) and similar books which I think can, in many ways, be more accurate than most astrology books. You might also make a practice of studying people in public places—buses, trains, parks, restaurants. Study them and try to analyze them. You'll have no way of verifying your ideas but it's valuable training.

• ∽ •

16

A Final Word

To repeat what I said at the end of the last chapter: Don't do a cold reading unless you absolutely have to. If necessary say, "I'm sorry but I'm just not in the mood for doing a reading right now. I'll be happy to give you one later, however." Clients will respect you much more for this honesty. And…sincerely try to help your client, as much as you possibly can.

Don't attempt to do medical diagnoses or prescribe medicine. You can certainly say something to the effect that "the old herbal cures were always considered very

Author Raymond Buckland and Peter Ingram in front of a beautiful Bow-Top vardo Ingram restored.

effective. Quite rightly so, to my mind." Here you are simply giving an opinion. But don't run the risk of being accused of practicing medicine without a license. Don't forget that the American Medical Association (AMA) is one of the federally encouraged monopolies!

Do *dis*claim supernatural powers. Let's face it, any "powers" that you are using are, in fact, quite *natural*.

Dukkerin', in the Gypsy fashion, is fun, constructive, and is essentially *practical*. None of the methods given in this book involves anything at all complicated or expensive. (No, you don't *have* to have a crystal ball, if you remember!) As with so much in the parapsychological field, *practice makes perfect*. Read for everybody. Read for people you know (in this way you can verify what you see) and also for people you don't know. Drag in the mail carrier, the newspaper delivery person, the door-to-door sales person—anyone you can. Read for them (they'll probably love it!) and see how well you do.

If you need the money or want to read professionally, don't let anyone tell you it's sinful! There is nothing wrong with being paid for a skill that you use to help others. Don't overcharge (you won't keep clients that way anyway) but don't sell yourself short either. At the same time, don't hesitate to not charge someone whom you feel needs a reading but cannot afford it.

The *Rom* are much maligned—as are the Wicca (see my *Buckland's Complete Book of Witchcraft*). The *Detroit News*, in April 1985, had a headline that screamed, "It's Gypsy Season...So Don't Get Gypped." As columnist Paul Dean pointed out in a *Los Angeles Times* article (October 5, 1986):

"That headline...would never have been published had it referred, for example, to Jews. The slur and the racism would be identical. Yet that Detroit headline inspired no public outrage, no editorial apologies or retraction." He goes on to say that the *Rom* remain the only ethnic minority against whom laws still operate and who are specifically named in those laws.

Gypsies are working to change this state. As Dean further reports: In 1985 "...the state Supreme Court ruled in favor of Gypsy fortuneteller Fatima Stevens (represented by attorney Barry Fisher) who had sued the city of Azusa claiming that its ban on fortunetellers violated her constitutional right of free speech. The ruling ended longstanding bans on fortune telling in other South Bay cities...The North American Chapter of the Gypsy Lore Society has formed a Romani Anti-Defamation League."

So the *Rom* are fighting back and, hopefully, receiving recognition and their rights. I sincerely hope that they will be able to continue their centuries-old tradition of *dukkerin'* without harassment.

Kushti bok,
Raymond Buckland

• ◢◣ •

LOOK FOR THE CRESCENT MOON

Llewellyn publishes hundreds of books on your favorite subjects! To get these exciting books, including the ones on the following pages, check your local bookstore or order them directly from Llewellyn.

ORDER BY PHONE

- Call toll-free within the U.S. and Canada, 1-800-THE MOON
- In Minnesota, call (612) 291-1970
- We accept VISA, MasterCard, and American Express

ORDER BY MAIL

- Send the full price of your order (MN residents add 7% sales tax) in U.S. funds, plus postage & handling to:

  Llewellyn Worldwide
  P.O. Box 64383, Dept. K092-2
  St. Paul, MN 55164–0383, U.S.A.

POSTAGE & HANDLING

(For the U.S., Canada, and Mexico)

- $4.00 for orders $15.00 and under
- $5.00 for orders over $15.00
- No charge for orders over $100.00

We ship UPS in the continental United States. We ship standard mail to P.O. boxes. Orders shipped to Alaska, Hawaii, The Virgin Islands, and Puerto Rico are sent first-class mail. Orders shipped to Canada and Mexico are sent surface mail.

International orders: Airmail—add freight equal to price of each book to the total price of order, plus $5.00 for each non-book item (audio tapes, etc.).

Surface mail—Add $1.00 per item.

Allow 4–6 weeks for delivery on all orders.
Postage and handling rates subject to change.

DISCOUNTS

We offer a 20% discount to group leaders or agents. You must order a minimum of 5 copies of the same book to get our special quantity price.

FREE CATALOG

Get a free copy of our color catalog, *New Worlds of Mind and Spirit*. Subscribe for just $10.00 in the United States and Canada ($30.00 overseas, airmail). Many bookstores carry *New Worlds*—ask for it!

Visit our web site at www.llewellyn.com for more information.

PRACTICAL COLOR MAGICK

Raymond Buckland, Ph. D.

Color magick is powerful—and safe. Here is a sourcebook for the psychic influence of color on our physical lives. Contains complete rituals and meditations for practical applications of color magick for health, success and love. Find full instructions on how to meditate more effectively and use color to stimulate the chakras and unfold psychic abilities. Learn to use color in divination and in the making of talismans, sigils and magick squares.

This book will teach all the powers of light and more. You'll learn new forms of expression of your innermost self, new ways of relating to others with the secret languages of light and color. Put true color back into your life with the rich spectrum of ideas and practical magical formulas from Practical Color Magick!

0-87542-047-8, 160 pp., illus., softcover   **$6.95**